REVISE EDEXCEL GCSE

History B
Schools History Project

REVISION GUIDE

Series Consultant: Harry Smith   Author: Kirsty Taylor

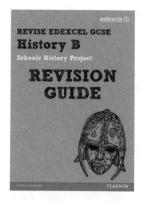

THE REVISE EDEXCEL SERIES
Available in print or online

Online editions for all titles in the Revise Edexcel series are available Summer 2013.

Presented on our ActiveLearn platform, you can view the full book and customise it by adding notes, comments and weblinks.

Print editions

History B Revision Guide	9781446905142
History B Revision Workbook Support	9781446905104
History B Revision Workbook Extend	9781446905074

Online editions

History B Revision Guide	9781446905166
History B Revision Workbook Support	9781446904985
History B Revision Workbook Extend	9781446905159

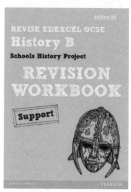

Print and online editions are also available for History A.

This Revision Guide is designed to complement your classroom and home learning, and to help prepare you for the exam. It does not include all the content and skills needed for the complete course. It is designed to work in combination with Edexcel's main GCSE History 2009 Series.

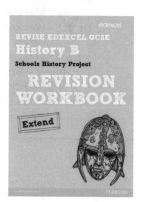

To find out more visit:
www.pearsonschools.co.uk/edexcelgcsehistoryrevision

ALWAYS LEARNING   **PEARSON**

Contents

> ✓ Make sure you know which topics you've studied – you only need to revise these!

A small bit of small print

Edexcel publishes Sample Assessment Material and the Specification on its website. This is the official content and this book should be used in conjunction with it. The questions in *Now try this* have been written to help you practise every topic in the book. Remember: the real exam questions may not look like this.

Medicine in c1350

Between 1350 and the Renaissance, ideas about the causes of disease were split between supernatural ideas and theories based on ideas from Ancient Greece and Rome.

The Four Humours

The Ancient Greeks thought everyone had a mix of four humours in their body. They believed people became ill when this mix was unbalanced, so to make people better they tried to put this balance right. These ideas continued well into the Middle Ages.

Theory of Opposites

In the second century AD, a doctor called Galen developed the idea of the Four Humours further. Besides bleeding and purging to get rid of excess humours, treatment based on his Theory of Opposites aimed to balance the humours by giving the patient the 'opposite' of their symptoms. For example, if you had too much phlegm (linked to water and cold) you should eat hot peppers.

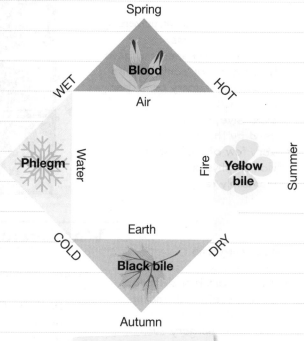

The Four Humours

The Christian Church

Christianity had great influence over medicine.

- People believed that God made them ill because He was displeased with them or testing their faith. This held back medical research, as people didn't believe there was a rational explanation for disease.

- On the other hand, the Church also taught that people should follow Jesus' example and care for the sick.

- Monasteries housed most books and the Church controlled education, so only ideas approved by the Church were taught.

- Galen's theories fitted Christian beliefs that the body had a soul and that all parts had been created by God to work together.

- The Church discouraged dissection and in general did not approve of people challenging ideas and authority.

Claudius Galen

Galen was a Greek doctor who worked in Ancient Rome. He wrote many books about his theories on human anatomy and treatments for disease. His influence lasted until the Middle Ages and his ideas became the basis of medical training.

Medical training

During the 12th century, universities set up medical schools where physicians were trained. Most teaching was done through books rather than practical experiments. Books included those by Christian and Muslim doctors but most were by Galen, whose ideas dominated.

Now try this

List **four** reasons why Galen's theories dominated medicine for well over 1000 years.

Treating the sick c1350

Physicians
- Medically trained at university and passed exams.
- Diagnosed illnesses and gave treatments, or sent patients to the apothecary or barber surgeon.
- Expensive, so mainly used by the wealthy.
- Very few of them, with women physicians incredibly rare.

Apothecaries
- Received training but no medical qualifications.
- Mixed medicines and ointments based on their own knowledge or directions of a physician.
- Cost money (but less than a physician).

Who treated the sick?

Barber surgeons
- No training.
- Carried out bloodletting, pulling teeth and lancing boils. Also cut hair!
- Did basic surgery such as amputating limbs (very low success rate).
- Cost less than a physician.

Monks and nuns
- Ran hospitals using Church donations. Cared for the elderly or poor (rather than people with common diseases). Some hospitals run for specific diseases such as leprosy, which kept sufferers away from others.
- Free.

Housewife physicians
- Usually a village 'wise woman' or lady of the manor who treated local people.
- Dealt with childbirth and common injuries/illnesses (broken bones, sore throats).
- Mixed herb and plant remedies. Also used charms and spells.
- The cheapest and most accessible option.

Treatments

Medicines and ointments were made from plants, herbs, spices and minerals, but only some of them worked. People prayed and went on pilgrimages hoping that God would cure them. Lucky charms or other superstitious cures such as powdered 'unicorn horn' were also used. Physicians often tried to restore the balance of someone's humours through bleeding, purging or the Theory of Opposites.

What physicians did

1 Commonly, physicians observed a patient's symptoms and checked their pulse, skin colour and urine (colour and taste!).

2 They consulted urine charts in their vademecum (handbook).

3 They then consulted zodiac charts to help diagnose the illness and to work out the best time to bleed the patient, if bloodletting was necessary.

4 They then either treated patients or sent them to a barber surgeon or apothecary.

Now try this

List **three** factors people might have considered before they sought medical help from someone.

The Black Death

In the 1340s, thousands of people were killed by a disease spreading across the world. That disease was 'the Black Death'. It reached Britain in 1348, killing about one-third of the population.

What was it?

Most historians today think this disease was bubonic plague, carried by fleas living on black rats, which brought the disease to different countries on trading ships. Bubonic plague is passed to humans when an infected flea bites them and the disease enters their blood.

How people thought the Black Death was caused	How people tried to avoid catching it
• Religion: God sent the plague as a punishment for people's sins. • Astrology: the position of Mars, Jupiter and Saturn was unusual at this time. • Miasma: bad air or smells caused by decaying rubbish. • Volcanoes: poisonous gases from European volcanoes and earthquakes carried in the air. • Four Humours: most physicians believed Galen's theory that all disease was caused by an imbalance in the Four Humours. • Outsiders: strangers or witches had caused the disease.	• Groups known as flagellants walked in procession to a church, praying and whipping each other to show God how sorry they were and ask for his mercy. • Praying and fasting. • Clearing up rubbish in the streets. • Smelling their toilets or other bad smells, in the belief this would overcome the plague. • Lighting a fire in the room, ringing bells or keeping birds flying so the air kept moving. • Carrying herbs and spices to avoid breathing in 'bad air'. • Not letting unknown people enter the town or village.

Symptoms

Symptoms of the Black Death included:

• swelling of the lymph glands into large lumps filled with pus (known as buboes)

• fever and chills

• headache

• vomiting, diarrhoea and abdominal pain.

Treatments

Treatments for the Black Death included:

• praying and holding lucky charms

• cutting open buboes to drain the pus

• holding bread against the buboes, then burying it in the ground

• eating cool things and taking cold baths.

Now try this

Give **three** examples of what people believed caused the Black Death, with corresponding ways they tried to avoid catching it.

The Renaissance

Medicine during the Middle Ages had changed little since Roman times. However, there were some new ideas that began to appear during the Renaissance.

The Renaissance

Renaissance is the term given to a period in European history meaning 'rebirth' as renewed interest in Ancient Greek and Roman ideas took hold. It saw the 'rebirth' of ideas and theories in medicine that people tested and challenged. It was also a great period of exploration when people from Europe 'discovered' new parts of the world bringing new plants from Africa and America that were useful in medicine.

The Reformation and The Royal Society

New religious ideas challenged the authority of the Catholic Church and other Christian Churches emerged. People were still very religious, but the Church's authority declined.

The Royal Society was established in Britain in 1660 by educated men who wanted to discuss new scientific ideas based on experiments, observation and recording/communicating the results.

New ideas about anatomy

Andreas Vesalius, Professor of Surgery at Padua University (Italy) proved many of Galen's ideas were incorrect. Vesalius drew the muscles, nerves, organs and skeleton of the human body from dissections. In 1543, he published *The Fabric of the Human Body*, which meant that others could learn about human anatomy.

New ideas about blood

William Harvey, a London doctor, discovered that Galen's ideas about blood were wrong. Harvey discovered that veins carry only blood, which was

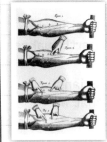

pumped through the body by the heart. He published his findings in 1628 in *An Anatomical Account of the Motion of the Heart and Blood in Animals*.

Technology

Developments in technology had a positive impact on medicine.

👍 Better microscope lenses helped discover bacteria.

👍 The invention of mechanical pumps helped people understand that the human body worked like a machine.

👍 Most importantly, the printing press was invented in the mid-15th century, allowing ideas and discoveries to be published and widely circulated.

Impact on medicine

However, discoveries during the Renaissance didn't improve treatments or life expectancy.

👎 Causes of diseases still not understood.

👎 Harvey's and Vesalius' ideas slow to be accepted.

👎 Medical teaching still mainly based on Galen's theories.

👎 Old treatment methods still used.

Now try this

Think about medicine and treatment during the Renaissance. Make a list of:

(a) things that changed

(b) things that stayed the same.

Industrialisation

The Industrial Revolution (c1750–c1900) saw huge changes in Britain.

Changing society

The invention of machines (a major factor in the Industrial Revolution) meant there was less work for people in the countryside. Towns and cities rapidly grew in population as people moved into them to work in the new factories. These changes had a big impact on people's health.

Causes of disease

Between 1750 and 1850 people came to believe more strongly in a rational, scientific explanation for disease. They thought disease was caused by:

- miasma – 'bad air' filled with fumes from rotting materials
- germs – produced by rotting animals and plants (spontaneous generation).

The problems

Poor quality housing – little ventilation, damp rooms.

Overcrowding and cramped living conditions – several families lived in one house.

Little fresh food in big towns and cities.

Drinking water often polluted by sewers.

Long working hours.

Many accidents in factories.

Poor working conditions – factories were often damp, with little ventilation.

Killer diseases

Thousands of people were killed by infectious diseases like:

- cholera
- diphtheria
- smallpox
- tuberculosis (TB)
- typhoid.

These were often caused by contaminated water and easily spread in poor living conditions. Cholera was particularly frightening because it spread very quickly and two-thirds of those who caught it died.

Treatments for cholera included:

- burning dead people's clothes and bedding
- praying and carrying lucky charms
- house cleaning using chloride of lime
- smoking cigars
- burning tar or vinegar to create smoke on the streets
- liquid or pills (patent medicines) that were supposed to cure all ills.

Now try this

Give **four** reasons why industrialisation led to more people dying from infectious diseases.

Breakthroughs, 1750–1900

Vaccinations and understanding germs were important breakthroughs. You will need to understand the reasons why.

Jenner and vaccination

Since the 1720s, doctors had been inoculating people against smallpox by infecting them with a mild version of the disease. This milder version could still kill. In 1796, Edward Jenner inoculated several people with pus from cowpox blisters, and found that they developed immunity to smallpox. Cowpox is not deadly.

- 1798: The Royal Society refused to publish Jenner's ideas, so he paid to print pamphlets explaining his work.
- 1802: Jennerian Society set up to promote vaccination.
- By 1804: 12 000+ people vaccinated.
- 1840: The Government began paying for vaccinations.
- 1853: The Government made vaccination compulsory.
- 1979: The World Health Organization (WHO) announced smallpox had been wiped out.

Opposition to Jenner

Many people opposed Jenner's work because:
- they thought it was wrong to give people an animal's disease
- it interfered with God's plan
- doctors lost money when the government offered vaccination free
- some doctors didn't vaccinate people properly so it didn't work.

Jenner's importance

Jenner's work proved that scientific methods could lead to a disease being wiped out. He saved the lives of millions! However:
- he didn't know why it worked
- the link between cowpox and smallpox was unique, so it didn't lead to other vaccinations
- other diseases were still killing people.

Germ Theory

In 1861, Louis Pasteur (a French chemist) published his germ theory, explaining that microbes (germs) in the air caused decay.

⬇

Robert Koch (who read Pasteur's work) linked bacteria to disease. He identified the specific microbe that caused anthrax in sheep, and the microbes causing TB and cholera. He discovered that chemical dyes stained bacteria, which made them easier to study under a microscope.

⬇

After work in 1879, Pasteur's team of scientists discovered that a weakened version of a disease-causing microbe could be used as a vaccine to create immunity from that disease.

Pasteur and Koch's importance

The work of Pasteur and Koch meant the true cause of certain diseases had been found. These techniques could identify other microbes causing diseases and then develop vaccines to prevent them and treatments to cure them. This showed the importance of scientists working in research teams. Publishing work in medical and scientific journals meant that the teams led by Pasteur and Koch could use each other's findings. However:

- it took time to identify specific microbes so prevention and treatment was not immediately possible
- the causes of some diseases (such as genetic conditions) were still unknown.

Now try this

List the factors that led to smallpox being wiped out.

Professionalising medicine

John Hunter encouraged medical students (including Jenner) to learn from their own research. A scientific approach to observing and experimenting began to be encouraged.

Improvements in medical training

- Teaching hospitals developed where students could observe doctors at work.
- Many students dissected bodies to understand human anatomy.
- Following Pasteur's germ theory, there was more emphasis on studying microbes and disease through microscopes.
- Training included how to use improved technology such as thermometers and stethoscopes to help diagnose illness.

Qualifications

Doctors needed a certificate from the Royal College of Physicians, the Royal College of Surgeons or the Society of Apothecaries. After 1815, the latter two set an exam to be passed before certificates were awarded. After 1858 all doctors had to be registered with the General Medical Council.

Midwives

Most midwives were women, but after forceps were introduced in the 17th century their numbers fell because they were not allowed the training necessary to use them. Instead 'men-midwives' became more common and treated the richer women.

Elizabeth Garrett Anderson

1 Women were not allowed to be doctors. Elizabeth (a nurse) defied the system and went to medical lectures until she was forced to stop. Then she studied privately.

2 The Society of Apothecaries did not bar women and Elizabeth passed their exam in 1865. After a court case, she was certified a doctor but the Society later changed its rules to prevent women qualifying.

3 She set up a medical practice in London and gained a medical degree at university in Paris. She helped set up the New Hospital for Women, and the London School of Medicine for Women.

4 She set an important precedent, and in 1876 women were allowed to go to university and obtain degrees.

Florence Nightingale

1 Nursing wasn't seen as a respectable job for women and there was little training.

2 Florence Nightingale attended the first nurses' training school in Kaiserwerth Hospital, Germany.

3 She was asked to lead a team of nurses at the military hospital in Scutari during the Crimean War (1854–56).

4 She believed that miasma caused disease, so emphasised hygiene, fresh air, good supplies and training for nurses. Her approach lowered the death rate at Scutari hospital from 42% to 2%.

5 Her work was widely reported in newspapers in Britain. She published books on nursing and hospital organisation and set up a training school for nurses/midwives.

Now try this

List the factors that improved doctors' training.

Treatment, 1750–1900

Improvements in treatment

1 People still used herbal remedies but had less access to plants so were more reliant on apothecaries. They also continued to use folk remedies based on superstition, but pills would soon take over.

2 Pills were made by hand until William Brockedon invented a machine in 1844 that standardised dosage and increased production speed.

3 Apothecaries and quack doctors sold patent medicines, advertised as cures for everything. However, their ingredients (such as lard and arsenic) didn't work or caused harm.

4 Money could be made from patent medicines, which encouraged growth of the pharmaceutical industry.

5 Jesse Boot turned one small shop into a chain of pharmacies.

6 Companies like Wellcome, Boots and Beecham financed chemical research to produce and sell their own brands of medicines.

7 By 1900 the government brought in regulations to prevent harmful ingredients being used in medicines.

8 New understanding of the causes of disease had little impact on prevention or treatment until the 20th century.

New hospitals (financed by charities and local councils) opened during the 19th century to look after the sick.

First cottage hospital (small buildings where nurses gave care and GPs prescribed treatment) opened in 1859.

Middle and upper classes could afford doctors to treat them at home.

Great Ormond Street Hospital, 1856

The elderly, sick or disabled poor were forced to enter workhouses.

Most hospitals tried to create a home atmosphere. Parents and visitors had to help nurses look after the patients.

Due to the work of reformers like Florence Nightingale, hospital cleanliness and organisation improved, and nurses were better trained. Pasteur's germ theory led to improved hygiene.

Nurses were given a more central role caring for patients and assisting doctors.

Great Ormond Street Hospital, 1875

Public pressure led to infirmaries (separate from workhouses) being set up for the poorest in society.

Specialist hospitals (such as asylums for the mentally ill and fever houses for infectious diseases) developed.

Now try this

Give **three** examples of ways in which hospitals had improved by the end of the 19th century.

Causes of disease since 1900

Understanding microbes

Throughout the 20th century scientists built on the research and findings of earlier years. They used techniques developed by Pasteur and Koch to discover more microbes that caused specific diseases. They also created vaccines to stop people catching these diseases. Knowledge of how microbes cause disease improved, which led to cures known as 'magic bullets' (see page 10 for more information).

Timeline

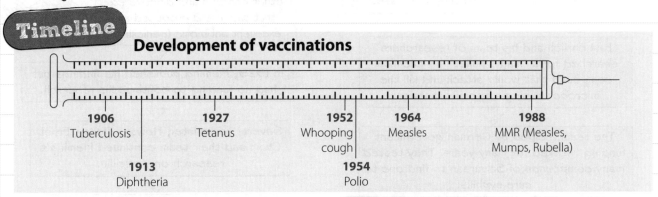

Development of vaccinations

1906	1913	1927	1952	1954	1964	1988
Tuberculosis	Diphtheria	Tetanus	Whooping cough	Polio	Measles	MMR (Measles, Mumps, Rubella)

Understanding genetics

During the 19th century, Mendel showed how human characteristics could be passed between generations.

⬇

In the 20th century new technology (electron microscopes, X-rays) let scientists analyse human cells in greater detail. They found that every cell in the body contains DNA – codes controlling the genes of each person.

⬇

Watson and Crick worked together on how the genetic codes of DNA fitted together.

⬇

They analysed X-ray crystallography by Maurice Wilkins and Rosalind Franklin at King's College Hospital (London) and eventually worked out the double helix structure of DNA (1953).

⬇

In 1990 James Watson led the Human Genome Project and started identifying and mapping every gene in human DNA.

Watson and Crick

James Watson was an American chemist and Francis Crick was a British physicist. Together, they studied the structure of DNA at the Medical Research Council (Cambridge University). In 1962 they received the Nobel Prize (along with Maurice Wilkins). Their work helped to improve our understanding of genetic conditions.

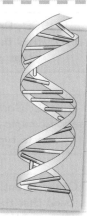

New possibilities

Discovering the structure of DNA and the work of the Human Genome Project, has led to impressive steps forward, such as:

- 👍 improved vaccines
- 👍 better insulin for diabetics
- 👍 new techniques for skin grafts
- 👍 better understanding of conditions such as Down's syndrome
- 👍 better understanding of whether people might develop certain types of cancer
- 👍 the discovery that stem cells can be grown into different cells.

Continuing research means that faulty genes could be corrected and genetic diseases could be prevented in the future.

Now try this

Give reasons why the discovery of the structure of DNA is so important for medicine.

Treatment since 1900

Magic bullets

Koch discovered that different chemical dyes stained specific microbes.

Behring discovered the body manufactures antitoxins that only attack the microbe causing a disease.

Paul Ehrlich and his team of researchers searched for a 'magic bullet' – a chemical compound that would attack and kill the microbe causing a specific disease.

The team, helped by German government funding, worked for many years. They tested many compounds of Salvarsan to find one to cure syphilis.

In 1909, Dr Hata joined the team and discovered they had rejected a compound that worked – the 606th!

In 1932, Gerhard Domagk developed the second magic bullet, Prontosil, which cured some types of blood poisoning.

Other scientists checking Domagk's work found that the key ingredient in Prontosil, sulphonamide, also cured pneumonia, scarlet fever and meningitis.

Penicillin

In 1928, Alexander Fleming noticed that bacteria in a Petri dish was being killed by a penicillium mould. He tested it on other bacteria and discovered that the mould produced an excellent antibiotic (penicillin).

In 1929, Fleming published his findings but had no funding to continue his research.

Several years later, Howard Florey, Ernst Chain and their team continued Fleming's research on penicillin.

It proved effective on mice, so they tested it on humans. Penicillin killed bacteria and therefore the infection – it was a miracle drug!

However, the mould had to be grown in huge quantities to be effective. British factories (damaged by bombing raids during the Second World War) and British drug companies were working flat out to produce other drugs needed for the war. In June 1941, Florey asked US drug companies for help. They refused, but when the US entered the war, and antibiotics were needed for injured soldiers, the US government offered funding.

The growth of the pharmaceutical industry

Chemical cures (magic bullets) and substances that cure bacterial infections (antibiotics) led to rapid growth in the pharmaceutical industry. Most chemical cures were injected at first, but technology developed in the late-19th century was now used to mass produce pills, so people could take them at home.

Blood transfusions

In 1901 Karl Landsteiner discovered there were four blood groups and a donor and a patient had to have the same blood group for transfusions to work. Blood clotted quickly, so donor and patient had to be together for transfusion. During the First World War, sodium citrate (which stopped clotting) was added, so blood could be stored for longer.

Now try this

List the factors that led to the development of (a) magic bullets and (b) penicillin as cures.

Health care since 1900 (1)

Gradual changes in health care began to help everyone access the medical help they needed.

Health care until 1948

Most health care was still done by women in the family using herbal or folk remedies, patent or other medicines bought from a chemist.

- Doctors charged for each visit, so were used mainly by the wealthy.
- Increasingly, doctors were either GPs who set up 'practices' and visited patients in their homes, or specialists who worked in large hospitals.
- Most cities had infirmaries, fever houses and asylums offering free basic care for the poor. They were run by local authorities and/or charities.

Government role

Between 1900–40 the government became increasingly involved in health care – partly because more than one-third of volunteers for the Boer War (1899–1902) were declared unfit.

Timeline

Government action

1907 Health visitors paid by government to help mothers

1919 Nursing Act: set up the General Nursing Council to promote high standards of care

1938 3000 died from diphtheria in the UK – led to a free immunisation programme in 1940

1902 Midwives Act: midwives to be trained and registered

1911 National Insurance Act – employees, employers and the government covered medical fees for employees

1919 Ministry of Health set up – the government gained an overview of health care across UK

Technology

Since 1900, technology has helped medicine in a variety of ways, such as:

- **research** – X-ray crystallography and electron microscopes
- **treatment** – pacemakers, dialysis machines, incubators, radiotherapy, hypodermic needles
- **diagnosis** – MRI, CT and ultrasound scans, X-ray machines, endoscopes
- **monitoring** – blood pressure kits, blood sugar level kits.

However, some of this is very expensive and needs specialised training to use.

Medical training

Training for doctors, nurses and most recently paramedics improved throughout the 20th century.

- Doctors' training involves a wide range of study, theory and practical work and takes about seven years. They may then choose to specialise.
- A nursing degree or diploma takes three years of theory plus practical work on different wards. Qualified nurses may then specialise, e.g. as a midwife.
- Doctors and nurses continue training in new techniques, drugs and technology.

Now try this

List reasons why many people continued to use folk remedies instead of more scientific treatments for the first few decades of the 20th century.

Health care since 1900 (2)

The increase in who could vote (especially after women won the vote in 1918) meant the government was more concerned about how poorer people could get health care.

What led to the setting up of the NHS in 1948?

The national Emergency Medical Service during the Second World War gave free treatment, proving that government control over health care could work.

During the Second World War, many families were shocked by the poverty of some of the evacuees they looked after. The war, in general, highlighted social inequality, which people wanted to change.

In 1942, the Beveridge Report identified disease as one of five major problems in British society.

It was accepted by the mid-20th century that government should involve itself in people's lives.

The NHS in 1948

Taxes funded a wide range of care:

- ✓ seeing a GP
- ✓ hospital care and operations
- ✓ health visitors for pregnant women and young children
- ✓ treatment by dentists and opticians
- ✓ ambulances and emergency treatment
- ✓ health care for the elderly.

Everyone in Britain could now access the same care, because all treatment was entirely free. Almost immediately, the nation's health improved, especially that of the poorest people.

NHS problems

Right from the start, the cost of running the NHS was much higher than expected. Therefore prescription charges for some items were introduced in 1951. Other charges followed, for example for opticians. Modern problems for the NHS include:

- people living longer (care for the elderly is extremely expensive)
- lack of nationwide availability for some drugs and treatments
- long waiting lists (so private medical insurance has grown).

The future of the NHS attracts great political debate.

Scientific issues

Scientific developments can sometimes have unforeseen consequences – e.g. thalidomide drugs in the 1960s. Some people object on moral and religious grounds to some kinds of research, such as embryo research. They are concerned about scientists 'playing God'. Additionally, some bacteria are now resistant to antibiotics, so stronger alternatives are needed.

Alternative medicine

In recent years, there has been increased interest in alternative treatments such as acupuncture and herbal remedies. As a result there are more shops selling alternative medicines and more practitioners giving alternative treatments. This may be because people do not like using chemical cures.

Now try this

Look at the last four topics (pages 9–12) and give reasons why, on average, people live much longer today than in 1900.

Medicine in Roman Britain

The Romans brought their ideas and systems with them to Britain after it became part of the Roman Empire in 43 AD.

Roman ideas and society

- There were major improvements in public health due to government-funded projects.

- Many different cultures and ideas from across the Empire spread to Britain – including the use of different herbal remedies.

- Many Greeks, including doctors, came to live and work in the Empire, bringing Greek ideas about medicine with them.

- More towns and cities grew up, which led to infection and diseases spreading more easily.

The army

Fitness and health were emphasised in the Roman Army. Forts usually contained well-equipped hospitals that treated injured soldiers. The hospitals provided training for surgeons and physicians, but few were open to the public so they would not have had an impact on the lives of ordinary people.

Ideas about disease

The Romans were happy to accept Greek ideas that disease was caused by, for example, the gods punishing them, curses from other people, bad air and dirt, or an imbalance in a person's humours.

Roman doctors

Roman doctors were not widely respected – many of them were foreign and often their treatments didn't work. This was because formal training wasn't required, so anyone could set up a practice.

Often, they learned medicine from working with another doctor or from books by Hippocrates or Galen.

Some might have trained in Alexandria in Egypt, where doctors could dissect human bodies (but that would have been very rare for doctors in Britain).

Most illnesses or injuries were treated by the father, using remedies passed down by his father.

Some remedies were used throughout the Empire and some were written down.

Treating the sick in Roman Britain

Prayers and offerings to gods were made.

The waters in Roman baths were believed to have healing qualities, so people visited them more often if they were unwell.

Celtic and Druid knowledge of herbs and plants was used in Britain to make medicines.

Now try this

Give examples that support the view that the Romans were more concerned with keeping healthy than in treating disease.

Public health in Roman Britain

Roman Britain saw the introduction of ideas that would help to improve public health.

Even though they didn't know why, Romans realised that cleanliness was linked to good health. Therefore, they built their towns in areas away from swamps and marshes, and tried to keep streets clean – though most towns had open drains.

Most towns had public baths that people visited every day to socialise and exercise. They also used the steam rooms, sauna and baths to clean themselves.

Skilled engineers built aqueducts and pipes, which brought clean water into towns. People also collected water from wells or bought it from water carriers. The rich had water piped into their houses.

A town in Roman Britain

Sewers were built to take away human waste from people's homes. Remains of these have been found in York and Colchester (among others).

The Roman Empire was wealthy, so people and the government had more to spend on infrastructure and education than other societies. The government provided the funding and resources (slaves, or the army in peacetime) to build and maintain public health projects such as sewers and baths.

Now try this

List reasons why public health provision in Roman Britain was so good compared to other societies.

Continuity c43 to c1350

There were changes in medicine and public health between the Roman period and c1350, but it is just as important to understand the things that stayed the same.

Hippocrates

Hippocrates was an Ancient Greek doctor. His ideas and books were very influential in Roman times and beyond. He dismissed the idea that gods caused disease – he believed there was a physical reason for illness, which needed a physical cure. Most of his treatments were based on diet, exercise and rest but he also used bleeding and purging to get rid of excess humours. He wrote the Hippocratic Oath, where doctors swore to respect life and prevent harm. His method of clinical observation – studying symptoms, making notes, comparing with similar cases, then diagnosing and treating – is the basis of the approach used today.

Continuity in treatments

There were few doctors in Roman and medieval Britain, and few people could afford to use them.

- Most treatment was given by a family member (usually the father in Roman times and the mother in the Middle Ages).
- Using prayers/religion to ask for a cure was common both before and after Christianity arrived in Britain.
- Remedies using plants and herbs were passed down by word of mouth or occasionally in writing.
- Doctors often prescribed treatments based on exercise, rest and diet.
- Treatments based on balancing the Four Humours, such as bloodletting or purging, or on Galen's Theory of Opposites, were also used throughout the entire period.

Galen

Galen was a Greek doctor who worked in Rome in the 2nd century AD. He wrote many books detailing his ideas, which were studied for the next 1000 years.

Galen carried out dissections on dead bodies (mainly animals). He then drew diagrams of them to explain human anatomy.

Galen and many others were convinced his ideas were right, and they dominated medicine for over 1500 years.

Galen developed Hippocrates' ideas. He mainly used bloodletting or purging to prevent illness.

Galen developed a Theory of Opposites to balance the humours and treat illness.

Galen operated on wounded gladiators. This increased his knowledge of anatomy.

Now try this

Jot down what features of medicine and public health largely stayed the same between c43 and c1350.

Questions may well focus on continuity rather than change.

Medieval medicine

Over 1000 hospitals were established in England and Wales in the Middle Ages. They were usually funded by charity and run by monks and nuns.

Hospitals

Hospitals cared for the sick rather than cured them. Their main focus was religion, and many hospitals were run by religious orders. Usually, people with infectious diseases or incurable conditions were not admitted. Some hospitals were built for specific infectious diseases (such as leper houses or lazars, which provided care and prevented infection spreading). Almshouses for the 'deserving' poor and elderly began to appear in the 14th century.

Doctors

When Roman administration ended, towns, wealth and numbers of doctors all decreased. Over time some monasteries became centres of learning, where formal medical training began. The first training was part of a bigger course in the 'arts' of rhetoric, geometry, astronomy and music. It took ten years to qualify and was very expensive. By the 12th century separate medical training had developed based on the ideas of Galen, along with translations of the writings of Muslim scholars. There were still very few doctors in Britain.

Most priests could read and write, giving them power in the local community. Senior churchmen were often advisers to the king.

Most people were happy to accept the Church's authority. Challenging its teachings/ideas was seen as going against God.

Most people strongly believed that sick people were being tested or punished by God. Praying and doing what He wanted was the only cure. Galen was not a Christian, but because his ideas fitted with those of the Church, it approved his teachings and kept his books.

Most books were kept in convents and monasteries, which meant Christianity could influence education and learning.

Caring for the sick was very important. Jesus and his followers had done this, so most hospitals were run by monks and nuns. However, the emphasis was on caring, not curing.

Many religious saints were associated with certain illnesses, so people prayed to the saint they thought could help them (e.g. St Blaise for a sore throat).

The Christian Church became increasingly important during the Middle Ages and dominated many aspects of life including medicine.

Now try this

In what ways did the Christian Church (a) help and (b) hinder medicine in the Middle Ages?

Medieval public health

The Romans left Britain in 410 AD, and this had huge consequences for public health. You will need to understand these consequences.

Medieval public health

As Britain separated into warring kingdoms, most people moved back to the countryside. Towns began to decay, as did public health systems. No one had the power or funding to build or maintain public health facilities. When towns grew again in the later Middle Ages, so did the problems with public health.

Poor hygiene

People in medieval times knew about the link between dirt and disease, but not how to solve the problem. Rubbish, dead animals and excrement were not removed from streets. Water from rivers was contaminated with dumped sewage and rubbish. Latrines were located above rivers or streams. Because of this, most people drank ale instead of water.

What was done?

Town councils and parliament tried unsuccessfully to resolve the problems.

Timeline

1281 Local authorities tried to ban pigs from London's streets

1347 Sanitary Act tried to keep streets cleaner; people could be fined for dropping waste

1388 Parliament tried to stop people dumping excrement in ditches and rivers. Town councils tried to improve fresh water supplies by running pipes or conduits into some towns and cities

Inequality

Not everyone lived in unhygienic conditions.

- Peasants weren't as badly affected because villages were not as crowded.

- Richer people could afford better standards, (such as privies [toilets], which kept waste away from living areas).

- Monasteries and convents had fresh water piped in and running water to remove waste.

- Many towns had public toilets and baths known as stewes.

Factors that influenced medieval public health

 Government

England was ruled by the king with support from the barons. Some kings were better than others at enforcing the laws and promoting public health. Power was also shared with the Church.

② War

Civil war disrupts everything in society – including improving public health or medical training. However, conflict could result in spreading new ideas.

Now try this

Look at this page and at page 14. Jot down reasons why Roman governments were more successful with public health than medieval governments.

Public health: problems, 1350–1750

Between 1350 and 1750 problems with public health provision increased because towns and cities were getting bigger. You need to know what these problems were and why they were hard to solve.

Problems

Rubbish, dead animals and human and animal excrement were dumped on streets and left there.

Rivers were often polluted and there was little clean water. Most people drank ale instead.

Poor sanitation caused health problems. Sewage often contaminated water.

Infectious disease

Outbreaks of infectious disease between 1350 and 1750 were frequent and deadly, partly because of poor public health provision. Local authorities tried several methods to deal with them, but they had little success because they didn't understand what caused disease.

During the 1665 plague in London:

- theatres were closed and large funerals were banned to stop crowds
- dogs and cats were killed
- barrels of tar were burned in streets
- every day, carts collected the dead who were buried in deep mass graves
- a household was boarded into its home for 28 days if one of them caught the plague
- days of fasting and prayers were ordered.

Toilets

- Only richer people had privies, which had padded seats over a bucket for their own family's use. Poorer people had to share, so several families would use one cesspit, which had a wooden seat above.

- Inside houses most people used chamber pots, which were emptied in drains in the street or sometimes just thrown out of the window.

- People paid nightsoil workers, or 'gong farmers', to empty cesspits (the contents would be sold to farmers to use as manure).

- In 1596 Sir John Harrington invented a water closet that used water to flush the sewage away. Many people ridiculed the idea, so it didn't develop properly for another 200 years.

Now try this

List examples of problems caused by poor public health provision between 1350 and 1750.

Public health: action, 1350–1900

People in medieval times knew there was some kind of link between dirt and disease so there were some attempts to deal with the problems. However, things were not the same everywhere or for everyone.

Dealing with problems

Town councils passed by-laws to make people keep streets clean and stop dumping things in rivers. Those who broke the rules were fined. Additionally, there were some successes in piping water into towns and cities.

Some towns had:

- public toilets, which stopped people relieving themselves in the streets
- public baths called stewes, where people bathed together.

Water in London

Two private investors tried to improve the city's poor water supply. In 1602 Edmund Colthurst began building an artificial river from the River Lee (Hertfordshire) to supply fresh water. His money ran out after just two miles! In 1609 Hugh Myddleton tried again and paid half the bills. The rest were paid by King James I. The project was finished in 1613, but couldn't keep up with demand. By 1750 most water was supplied by private companies, piped direct to homes or to standpipes on street corners.

Why wasn't more done?

The link between dirt and disease wasn't proven until 1861. People didn't worry about hygiene because they believed God caused disease. They didn't want rates (local taxes) spent on public health provision. Health wasn't seen as something for the government to be involved in.

EXAM ALERT!

Remember that until the 19th century most action on public health was done by local authorities rather than the national government.

Students have struggled with this topic in recent exams – **be prepared!** ResultsPlus

Role of government

Government is essential because it can pass laws forcing people to change their behaviour. There were some signs that the government was trying to prevent diseases and health problems after 1750.

In 1750, the government made gin more expensive to improve:

- health among the poor who were drinking lots of cheap gin
- the economy, because drunk people didn't work so hard.

GIN

In 1853, the government made smallpox vaccination compulsory. Then, in 1871 it made local authorities register all those vaccinated. This dramatically reduced deaths from smallpox.

Now try this

Give reasons why public health provisions often didn't work between 1350 and 1900.

Industrial diseases

Urban diseases

The Industrial Revolution (during the 18th and 19th centuries) caused huge growth in towns as people moved closer to work in new factories. Low wages meant several families shared low-quality housing. There were no laws to provide sewers, fresh water or toilets, or to remove rubbish. Infectious diseases spread more rapidly. In 1831, the appearance of cholera in Britain for the first time, put pressure on the local authorities to take action. Cholera could kill someone within a day and spread rapidly through communities. The first outbreak in Britain killed thousands in just a few weeks.

Edwin Chadwick

Chadwick was secretary to the Poor Law Commission, which was in charge of all workhouses in Britain. He was hard-working but sometimes arrogant, so few people liked him. He undertook a survey of conditions in working-class areas of towns to work out how to reduce the taxes needed for workhouses. In 1842 he published the results, entitled *The Sanitary Conditions of the Labouring Population*. He got a lot of attention, and some criticism.

- There was a belief in laissez-faire at the time; a belief that the government should not interfere in people's lives.
- People also believed that government should not interfere in business (government sanitation schemes reduced water companies' profits).
- People did not want to pay towards improving conditions for others who could not pay themselves.

Chadwick's opponents were nicknamed the 'Dirty Party'. Little was done until another outbreak of cholera in 1848 led to the Public Health Act.

Timeline

Cholera outbreaks

1848–49
Over 53 000 died

1865–66
Over 14 000 died

1831–32
Over 26 000 died

1853–54
Over 20 000 died

Chadwick's Report

Edwin Chadwick

The problem
Many people are ill because they live in unsanitary, overcrowded conditions. Workhouses take in those too old, weak or ill to work and look after themselves. They are run by local authorities with taxpayers' money, and the cost is high.

The solution
People need access to clean water. Sewers should be improved, and people's sewage and rubbish removed. This will reduce illness and admission to workhouses, so will save money in the long run.

Now try this

Give reasons why some people were against the ideas in Chadwick's report.

Government action

Public Health Act, 1848

This set up a General Board of Health with Chadwick as one of three commissioners. The Act allowed, but did not force, town councils to:

- set up their own local Board of Health
- appoint a local medical officer
- organise the removal of rubbish
- build a sewer system.

Only one third of towns set up a Board of Health. Even fewer appointed a medical officer. The Act was only temporary and the General Board of Health was abolished in 1858.

John Snow

Snow was a doctor and surgeon who had a theory that cholera was spread through water, not 'bad air' (as most people believed). When cholera broke out again in 1854 he mapped all the deaths in one area and found a strong link to one water pump on Broad Street. He removed the handle from the pump so people couldn't collect water from it and the number of deaths in that area fell dramatically. His work seemed to prove there was a link between water and cholera, but still nothing was done.

Steps to action

William Farr studied the statistics on births and deaths the government had been collating since 1837. He published details of death rates and causes in different places. (This is an example of the importance of individuals and of a scientific approach to solving problems of public health.)

→

John Snow's investigation of the Broad Street water pump showed that death rates varied according to where different water companies got their water from. (This is an example of the importance of individuals and of a scientific approach to solving problems of public health.)

→

London's 'Great Stink' (1858) persuaded the Metropolitan Board of Works to build an expensive new sewer system. (This is an example of the importance of technology in improving public health provision.)

Pasteur's germ theory published in 1861 showed how disease was really spread and how important hygiene was. (This is an example of the importance of scientific knowledge in solving problems of public health.)

→

In 1867 most working-class men in towns got the vote and wanted politicians to take action. (This is an example of the importance of the role of government in improving public health.)

→

Central government passed laws, and local authorities funded and carried out changes that improved conditions. By 1875 local councils had to ensure that:
- clean water was provided
- streets were paved
- rubbish was collected
- sewers were built
- slum housing was demolished
- food in shops was of good quality.

Now try this

Give **two** ways in which Edwin Chadwick was influential in changing public health provision and **two** ways in which he made little difference.

Public health since 1900

Reforms 1900-1948

In 1905, the Liberal government took action in response to worrying health trends.

- Surveys by Charles Booth and Seebohm Rowntree showed how difficult it was for the working classes to afford decent housing and food.
- One third of volunteers to fight in the Boer War (1899–1902) did not pass the army health tests (nearly 90% failed the test in slum areas of northern cities).

It was still difficult to get reforms passed because they were expensive and many people objected to increasing government involvement in people's lives.

Timeline

1902 Midwives Act – all midwives had to be trained and registered

1906 Free school meals for poor children

1907 School Medical Service

1907 Health visitors to check on mothers and young children

1908 Old Age Pensions Act

1911 National Insurance Act – health insurance scheme giving access to medical treatment for workers, plus limited sick pay and unemployment support

1919 Ministry of Health – gave overview of health care throughout the UK

1919–39 More hospitals brought under control of local authorities

1934 Free milk at primary schools for poor children

1940 Free diphtheria vaccinations at health clinics

The NHS

The Second World War made people aware of the importance of government involvement in health care. Plans were made for a National Health Service, which was set up in 1948 by Health Minister Aneurin Bevan. This gave free access to health care for everyone and was a landmark event for public health in Britain.

Aneurin Bevan

Bevan faced opposition to the NHS from doctors who worried they would lose independence and money. He put pressure on them by publicising his ideas and persuading people to register as NHS patients, but also agreed they could still have private patients. He resigned in 1951 when prescription charges were introduced.

Prevention measures

Since 1948 the government has taken more action to prevent people getting ill:

- ✓ funding more vaccinations (polio in 1952) and tests (cervical cancer in 2008)
- ✓ better disposal of rubbish and sewage
- ✓ laws reducing air and water pollution (e.g. 1956 Clean Air Act)
- ✓ laws improving health and safety at work
- ✓ environmental health officers inspecting food outlets.

Health education

Since 1948, the government has funded posters, leaflets and advertisements to raise awareness of illnesses. These have had some success: the 1980s 'AIDS: don't die of ignorance' campaign reduced cases of HIV infection.

Laws have also been passed to influence people's behaviour and improve health – such as a ban on advertising tobacco products, high tax on cigarettes and banning smoking in public places.

Now try this

List **four** factors that led to improvements in public health in the 20th century.

Crime and punishment in 1450

You need to know the types of crime and how they were punished in 1450 so that you can see what changed and what stayed the same from 1450 to 1700 (where this section ends).

Medieval crimes and punishments

The people who made laws were those with power and wealth. Crimes that threatened this power and wealth were thought of as serious. They were punished by death. The more serious the crime, the more horrible the death penalty.

Crime	How common	How serious	Usual punishment
Stealing very small amounts of money, goods or food	Very	Not serious	Fine, stocks or pillory
Selling goods at the wrong prices	Very	Not serious	Fine
Selling poor quality goods	Very	Not serious	Fine, stocks or pillory
Assault	Rare	Fairly serious	Stocks or pillory, whipping
Blasphemy (taking God's name in vain)	Fairly	Fairly serious	Branding
Theft of money or goods worth two days' wages or more	Very	Very serious	Hanging
Arson	Rare	Very serious	Hanging
Rape	Rare	Very serious	Hanging
Murder	Rare	Very serious	Hanging
Heresy (not following official beliefs of the Church)	Rare	Very serious	Burning at stake
Treason	Very rare	Extremely serious	Hanging, drawing and quartering

Justice

Most people lived in small villages with a manor court which met frequently. By 1450 they mostly used a jury of twelve freemen to decide if someone was guilty. People accused of more serious crimes were sent from manor courts to the royal court, which used trial by jury and could sentence people to the death penalty. Church courts dealt with priests, monks and nuns accused of crimes or ordinary people who had broken Church rules (moral 'crimes' such as adultery or not paying their tithes).

Catching medieval criminals

There were no police. The community was responsible for finding criminals through tithings (groups of ten freemen), except clergy and knights, who were responsible for each other.

- If one of these men was accused of a crime, the rest brought that person to justice or paid a fine to the victim.
- If a crime was committed, any bystanders were expected to shout and chase the criminal (known as the 'hue and cry').

Now try this

Describe medieval attitudes to punishment, considering what kinds of punishment were used and why.

Crime, 1450–1750

British society from 1450 to 1750 saw many changes, including an increase in crimes – both traditional kinds and new kinds created by new laws.

A changing society

During the Middle Ages most people had lived in small villages where they knew everyone else. It was rare for anyone to leave. Many people were villeins, tied to the lord of the manor's land.

Factors affecting crime rates

The number of people committing crimes rose when:
- prices and unemployment were high
- taxes were increased during wars.

A strong government meant lower crime as criminals were more likely to be punished.

Why did crime increase?

Change in society		Led to 'new' crimes or increase in existing crime
Increase in population and decline of feudalism meant more people moved to urban areas, so towns and cities got bigger.		More street criminals and thieves – known as footpads.
Increased unemployment meant more people moved around looking for work.		Led to more people begging, which became a crime in the 16th century.
Trade between towns grew, leading to roads being improved between 1700 and 1750.		Led to a new type of thief – highwaymen robbing travellers on the roads.
The end of feudalism led to a reduction in common land because land owners fenced it off.		Led to an increase in poaching as landowners restricted who could hunt on their land.
Changes in people's religious beliefs and the religion of the monarch.		Led to more people committing 'heresy' during the 16th century.
More trade restrictions (in 1614, exporting wool became illegal and tax on tea and brandy increased in the 18th century).		Created the new crime of smuggling: people imported and or exported illegal goods or goods that were heavily taxed.

Now try this

Complete a table with 'Crimes that remained the same or did not increase' in the left column and 'Crimes that increased and new crimes that developed' in the right column.

Begging and treason

Begging was a new crime. Treason was an old crime that became more common after 1485.

New crimes

Laws can change because of pressure from new rulers or ordinary people. These new laws sometimes create new crimes. Begging is an example of a new crime in this period.

Rulers under threat

Rulers who felt they were under threat would punish crimes very harshly to deter other criminals. Treason was one crime that was taken very seriously.

Begging

> Increased unemployment and no system to help the needy meant higher numbers of beggars in the late 15th and 16th centuries.

> Beggars were seen as a threat to society. They were hated and feared, and people resented paying out to support them.

Laws were passed against begging.
- Vagabonds and Beggars Act (1494): beggars were put in the stocks for three days and nights, then sent back to where they were born or most well known.
- In 1531 beggars were classed as:
  - either 'deserving' (sick or injured), who were given a badge and allowed to beg
  - or 'sturdy beggars', who were considered lazy, and therefore punished.
- Vagrancy Act, 1547: beggars were forced to work, and could be whipped and branded. The Act was repealed because it was impossible to enforce.

Treason

Treason charges were more common in this period because:

> Henry VII (Henry Tudor) taking power in 1485, is a good example.

- there were more disputes over who should be king, e.g. during the Wars of the Roses (1455–85)

- some people wanted a monarch with a different religion.

> The 'Gunpowder Plot', when some Catholics tried to kill the Protestant James I, is a good example.

At this time, treason was punished by public hanging, drawing and quartering (to deter others). Nobles were usually beheaded.

Guy Fawkes

On 5 November 1605, a few Catholics who wanted a Catholic monarch planned to kill the King and Members of Parliament at the state opening of Parliament. The plotters were betrayed and one of them, Guy Fawkes, was caught in a cellar of the Houses of Parliament guarding barrels of gunpowder. When the plotters were found, they were all hanged, drawn and quartered.

EXAM ALERT!

Make sure you are clear about who was of which religion. The Catholic plotters tried to kill the Protestant King James I.

Students have struggled with this topic in recent exams – **be prepared!**   ResultsPlus

Now try this

List reasons why:

(a) begging became a crime.

(b) the charge of treason became more common between 1450 and 1750.

Punishment, 1450–1750

As towns grew bigger, more crimes occurred. This worried those who made the laws. As a result, they increased the number of crimes carrying the death penalty as they thought that it would help to reduce crime.

Types of punishment

Punishments were usually physical, using the equipment below. The public could watch – to shame the criminal and deter others.

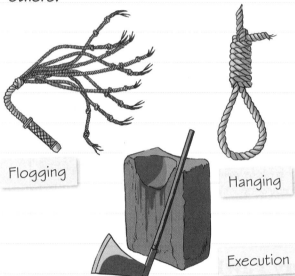

Flogging

Hanging

Execution

The Bloody Code

Between 1688 and 1823 the number of crimes punishable by death rose from 50 to more than 200. This period became known as the 'Bloody Code'. Stealing a rabbit or damaging a tree became hanging offences. The aim was to frighten people so they wouldn't commit crimes. However, it didn't work. Fewer people were hanged in the 18th century than the 17th because juries found people 'not guilty' to avoid them being given the death penalty.

New punishments

- Local judges began to build Houses of Correction (the first prisons) where beggars were sent from 1576.
- Some petty or political criminals were sent as labourers to English colonies from the late 17th century (transportation).

Policing

There was no national system for catching criminals.

- Watchmen, or 'Charlies' (set up under Charles II), were paid to patrol London.
- Unpaid parish officials called constables arrested beggars and petty criminals.
- Thief takers were paid by the victim of a crime to catch the criminal and bring them to justice.

Jonathan Wild

Wild was a famous thief taker who claimed to have had over 60 thieves hanged, and returned stolen goods for the rewards.
- However, he was actually a criminal who ran a successful gang of thieves.
- He caught 'thieves' who were either rivals or gang members who wouldn't obey him.
- He was hanged in 1725.

Trials and juries

Minor cases were heard locally by one or two Justices of the Peace. More serious crimes were heard by groups of JPs with local men serving on a jury. The most serious were heard by royal judges who were the only ones able to pass a death sentence.

Inequality

Punishments varied depending on class and gender – commoners were treated differently to nobles, women differently to men and priests differently to ordinary people.

Now try this

Jot down the aims of punishment during the period 1450–1750.

Crime, 1750–1900 (1)

You need to know how changes in society and the media played a role in the crime rate and perceptions of crime.

 Changes in society

The move from agriculture to industry and from countryside to town had already begun but increased dramatically after 1750. Crime continued to increase until 1850, when it began to fall. There were some new crimes but most crime continued to be petty theft.

 The media

This period saw the development of cheap illustrated newspapers, which were very popular. For the first time, instances of crime, especially violent crime, were reported all over Britain. This made many people more aware and afraid of crime.

The impact of industrialisation

Industrialisation meant the arrival of machines and steam power for manufacturing, agriculture and transport.

↓

Impact on work and society
- Huge factories in towns and cities, rather than people working at home in their villages.
- Workers replaced by machines in some industries and agriculture.
- Urbanisation as people moved into towns and cities to find work. The poor settled in poor areas where huge slums developed.
- Industrialisation made some people very rich but meant extreme poverty for others.
- Government brought in new laws or used existing ones to raise money and control people.

Urbanisation

↓

Impact on crime
There was an increase in crimes such as:
- street theft and burglary
- drunk and disorderly behaviour
- prostitution (including child prostitution)
- rioting, public disorder and protest
- smuggling of illegal goods.

→

These crimes increased for a number of reasons:
- Travel and movement into towns meant it was harder to keep track of people.
- Larger towns made it easier to escape being caught.
- Some criminals became 'professional' operatives within dens or gangs of thieves.
- Extreme poverty created 'survival' crimes such as stealing food.
- The poor worked alongside the rich; the poor felt discontented, while the rich sometimes felt threatened by the poor.

Now try this

What crimes were people in extreme poverty likely to commit?

Crime, 1750–1900 (2)

Due to urbanisation, crimes against property rose in this period but it's important to also revise what happened to crimes against the person and authority.

Crimes against authority

Treason charges fell, but there were other threats. The French Revolution in 1789 made the government and upper classes afraid that something similar would happen in Britain. Many people wanted reforms like the right to vote and the right to strike. The government was very hard on protestors but agreed to some reforms in the late nineteenth century, which improved conditions and reduced protests.

Crimes against the person

Violent crimes decreased during this period, even though many people at the time thought differently!

- In the 1850s there was concern about 'garrotters' who used chloroform or part-strangled people to rob them.
- The horrific Jack the Ripper murders in 1888 were widely reported in newspapers and caused widespread fear.

Examples of crimes against authority

Example of threat	How the government dealt with threat
Groups who wanted the right to vote and reform of Parliament met at St Peter's Fields, Manchester. 	Soldiers were sent in to arrest the leaders, but behaved violently leading to deaths and injuries in what is known as The Peterloo Massacre. New laws were passed banning unauthorised meetings and increasing punishments for criticising the government.
Group of farm workers who formed a trade union to stop wage cuts in Tolpuddle, Dorset (1833).  A CONTEMPORARY IMPRESSION OF THE TOLPUDDLE MARTYRS	The farm workers were arrested for 'swearing secret oaths' and transported to Australia for seven years. In 1836, the government were forced to release the 'Tolpuddle Martyrs' after huge protest meetings, marches and petitions.

Smuggling

Smuggling increased during the period 1740–1850 because the tax on imported goods was so high. Smugglers made large profits by bringing these goods into the country illegally (without paying tax) and selling them on cheaply. Mounted customs officers tried to stop smuggling and prosecute smugglers. They found it difficult because of the large area of coast to patrol. Taxes were cut in 1850 and smuggling decreased.

Remember that many people thought smugglers were heroes who brought them cheap goods. They thought the government was being unreasonable. Lots of people were involved in smuggling:
- the smugglers themselves
- those who traded with smugglers
- those who bought smuggled goods
- those who hid smuggled goods
- those who protected the smugglers by giving them alibis.

Now try this

List reasons why smuggling laws were difficult to enforce in the 18th and 19th centuries.

Policing, 1750-1900

Policing was beginning to change. You will need to know what these changes were and the main people involved.

Policing 1749-1829

Watchmen continued to patrol cities on foot at night and parish constables dealt with petty crime. Soldiers were used to put down riots and large protests across the country. There were some changes in London though, as from 1749 the Bow Street Runners tracked down criminals and stolen property. From 1754 the Bow Street Horse Patrols patrolled the streets.

The Fielding Brothers

Henry Fielding became chief magistrate at Bow Street Court in 1748. He and his half-brother John set up the Bow Street Runners – men paid by the magistrates to catch criminals – to increase the number of criminals sent to court and tried. The brothers also set up the Bow Street Horse Patrols. However, this was less successful because crime was dramatically increasing in London and they didn't have enough patrols.

Robert Peel

As Home Secretary, Peel persuaded Parliament to pass the Metropolitan Police Act (1829), which set up London's first police force. He ended the 'Bloody Code' by reducing the number of death penalty offences. He also tried to reform the prison system with the Gaols Act, 1823.

EXAM ALERT!

Make sure you know the difference between the Bow Street Runners and the Metropolitan Police. The Runners did not aim to prevent crime, just catch the criminals.

Students have struggled with this topic in recent exams – **be prepared!** ResultsPlus

Set up in London in 1829. Became compulsory in 1856 for all counties and boroughs to have a police force based on the London model. These forces were independent.

Recruits carefully selected and well trained. It was a full-time and fairly well paid job.

Members had a uniform so they could be identified (and didn't look like soldiers).

The Metropolitan Police

Detective department set up in 1842. As well as patrolling, the force now began to solve crimes. Many crimes were not solved, but the department was seen as successful.

Focused on patrolling areas where crime was high. Successfully reduced street crime and disorder.

Not popular at first, but soon recognised by the public as being honest and trustworthy.

Now try this

Jot down **three** reasons why the Metropolitan Police Act managed to reduce the crime rate.

 This Act is very important so make sure you know why it was introduced and what effects it had.

Punishment, 1750–1900

Attitudes to punishment continued to change, and you will need to be familiar with all the details.

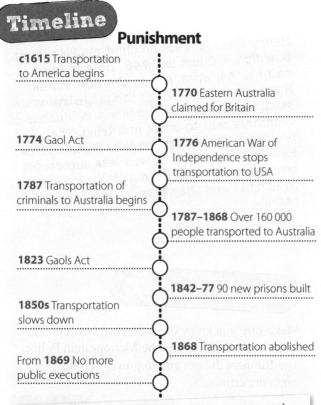

Timeline

Punishment

c1615 Transportation to America begins

1770 Eastern Australia claimed for Britain

1774 Gaol Act

1776 American War of Independence stops transportation to USA

1787 Transportation of criminals to Australia begins

1787–1868 Over 160 000 people transported to Australia

1823 Gaols Act

1842–77 90 new prisons built

1850s Transportation slows down

1868 Transportation abolished

From **1869** No more public executions

The death penalty became less common in this period. After 1869 public executions were banned and people were hanged inside prisons.

Transportation to Australia

Petty crime was growing, but so was the feeling that execution was too harsh a punishment. Transportation was used as an alternative to hanging because it removed criminals from British society and still acted as a deterrent. It also provided free labour to build infrastructure in Australia.

However, transportation ended because:

1 Australia no longer needed forced labourers (the discovery of gold made it an attractive place to go) and it didn't want 'criminals'.

2 Some felt it was too expensive and not a strong enough deterrent for crime. Others felt it was too harsh for both the criminals and their families.

3 More prisons had been built and prison was increasingly used instead of transportation.

Prison reformers

John Howard's work led to the 1774 Gaol Act, which suggested how health and sanitation in prisons could be improved. Elizabeth Fry began visiting women in Newgate prison in 1813. She set up education classes to reform female prisoners. She also got them better food and clothes, and treated prisoners with kindness and respect.

Prisons

Until the late 18th century, prisons were used mainly for debtors. As the death penalty became less acceptable, other criminals were increasingly imprisoned too as it removed them from society and acted as a deterrent without killing them. In the 19th century, prison systems were developed aimed at reforming prisoners so they wouldn't re-offend. The Separate System and Silent System isolated prisoners from each other to encourage self-reflection and repentance. These systems were expensive and some prisons continued to use hard labour and punishments instead.

Peel's prison reforms

1823 Gaols Act: paid gaolers, work and basic education, prison inspections, visits by chaplains and doctors, women gaolers for women prisoners.

1830s: prisoners given clean, separate cells and more work. New prison-building programme.

Now try this

Jot down how attitudes towards punishment changed during the period 1750–1900.

 You will need to know about changing attitudes.

Crime since 1900 (1)

As Britain developed and changed, so criminals saw new and different ways of committing crimes.

Changing society

In the 20th century, Britain developed into a society that was:

- multicultural, with people of different races and religions
- more prosperous
- more equal, as the position of women changed
- high-tech and fast moving.

These changes had a big impact on crime and punishment. For example, new technology meant that new crimes developed, as did new ways of enforcing law and catching criminals.

Common crimes

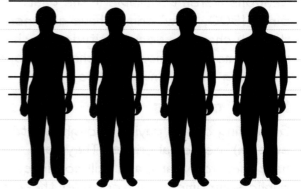

| Driving offences/ car theft | Vandalism/ burglary | Assault/ mugging | Petty theft/ antisocial behaviour |

Crime rates

Rates of crime rose between 1900 and 1992. Some suggest the main reason for this was that people had less respect for others and for authority. However, there are other factors to consider.

- Far more actions became classed as crimes.
- Victims of crime became more likely to report it.
- Ways of recording crime improved.

Crime reached a peak in 1992 and has been falling since then.

New laws

During the 20th and 21st centuries more actions have become crimes. The reasons for this are the same as in the past.

- The government makes new laws to deal with things it is worried about.
- Public opinion pressures the government into creating new laws.

Changing attitudes and opinions play a large part. Some crimes of the 20th century did not last long. Others may be more permanent.

Computer hacking

Sex discrimination ——— | **Some new crimes in the 20th century** | ——— Race crime

Traffic crime

Now try this

Jot down reasons why **(a)** traffic crime and **(b)** race crime became crimes in the 20th century.

Crime since 1900 (2)

Some 'new' crimes are very similar to old crimes but they use new technology.

New or old?

Theft has always been a common crime. However, computers and modern transport have created new ways to steal. Violence too is centuries old, although modern weapons weren't available in the past. Since 1900, 'new' crimes have emerged through changing social attitudes (such as race crimes) and modern technology (such as driving while using a mobile phone).

Social crimes

Smuggling or not paying enough tax (tax evasion) are social crimes. They have happened for years, and still continue. The public sometimes don't consider these as crimes at all, so they may not be treated seriously.

Terrorism

Terrorism is not new but modern weapons, transport and communications mean that more ordinary people are at risk (though the risk is extremely low).

On 7 July 2005 four suicide bombers, who claimed to be members of Al Qaeda, attacked central London. Three bombs went off on underground trains and one on a bus. Fifty-two people were killed and 770 injured.

New crimes?	Old crimes
Smuggling illegal drugs and legal items (such as cigarettes and alcohol) without paying tax.	Smuggling illegal items and legal items without paying tax has happened for centuries.
People trafficking – 'selling' people for prostitution and forced labour.	'White slave trade' ('selling' women and children into prostitution in the 19th century).
Stealing money or gaining bank details from people through fraud using modern communication forms.	Stealing or conning money from someone using fraud has happened for hundreds of years.
Antisocial behaviour.	Antisocial behaviour has happened for years.

 Examples are creating a disturbance, and being drunk and disorderly.

The media

The media has always been interested in reporting shocking crimes, which has always given the impression that crime is rising and puts us at risk. Terrorism is one modern risk which is extremely low but seems higher because of media coverage.

EXAM ALERT!

In your answer to questions about 'new' crimes, don't just give a list of old or new crimes. Think about the nature of the crime and how it is committed to explain what makes it old or new.

Students have struggled with this topic in recent exams – **be prepared!**   ResultsPlus

Now try this

Give **two** examples each of (a) modern 'social crimes', (b) genuinely 'new' crimes since 1900 and (c) 'new' crimes that are actually 'old' crimes using modern technology.

 The best answers give examples.

Policing since 1900

These days, policing is about co-operation, solving crime and catching criminals.

Technology

Technology has had a big impact on preventing, discovering and prosecuting crime since 1900.

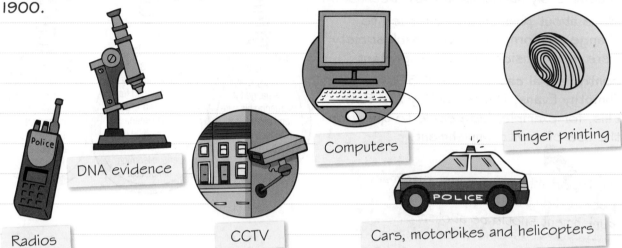

Radios   DNA evidence   CCTV   Computers   Cars, motorbikes and helicopters   Finger printing

Changes in policing

Much of modern policing is about preventing crime as well as catching criminals. The police work with different forces and other agencies across the UK and worldwide.

✓ Motorised transport means that police can reach crimes faster. However, it also means fewer police officers on the street, which some people don't like.

✓ Some police officers are now armed and look more like soldiers.

✓ The modern police force includes women and officers from different ethnic groups.

✓ In 1982 Neighbourhood Watch groups were set up in the UK. These groups help people prevent and detect crime in their neighbourhood. The police often work closely with these groups to advise and educate.

✓ In 2002 Police Community Support Officers were introduced.

Terrorism

This has been a challenge for the police since the late nineteenth century. During the 20th century, groups such as the IRA carried out terrorist attacks in Britain. In the 21st century, the threat of terrorism comes mainly from extreme religious groups such as Al Qaeda. Terrorism has had a big impact on modern policing.

• The police work closely with international forces and secret intelligence services to prevent attacks and gain evidence to prosecute those planning them. They use informers and undercover police, and monitor the communications of terrorist suspects.

• Suicide attacks are difficult for the police to deal with as the attackers don't worry about punishment or who they target. They want to die and kill many others in the process. They are difficult to detect because they work individually or in very small cells.

Now try this

For each item shown in the 'technology' section, give an example of how this has helped the police since 1900.

Punishment since 1900

Methods of punishment have changed over the centuries – including during the 20th century.

End of capital punishment

Capital punishment was last used in 1964. It was completely abolished in 1999 because:

- ideas about punishment continued to change – reform and paying back society were now considered more important
- controversial cases in the 1950s (Timothy Evans, Derek Bentley and Ruth Ellis, for example) led people to question the use of capital punishment.

It's important to remember that many people didn't agree that capital punishment should be abolished.

Controversial cases

1950: Timothy Evans was hanged for murdering his wife and baby. Later evidence proved he didn't do it.

1953: Derek Bentley was hanged for murdering a policeman, even though he didn't fire the gun and had serious learning difficulties.

1955: Ruth Ellis was hanged for murdering her boyfriend after he had violently abused her for years.

Prison

The use of prison as a punishment continued to increase after 1900 with many changes.

- Different prisons (e.g. open, high security) cater for different types of criminals.
- Since 1907, prisoners have been released on probation – they are watched by probation officers and put in prison if they re-offend.
- In 1948 hard labour and corporal punishment in prisons were abolished.
- Separate 'prisons' have been established for young people. Borstals were set up in the early 1900s. They used work and education to try to reduce re-offending rates. Today's Young Offenders Institutions have high re-offending rates.
- There has been a recent rise in female prisoners, although still only 6% of all prisoners are women.
- Women's and men's prisons differ (e.g. women can spend more time with their children).

New punishments

New types of punishment have devloped in the last two decades.

- Community sentences – working on community projects, for example.
- Treatment programmes for criminals with drug and alcohol problems.
- ASBOs.
- Electronic tagging.

Rehabilitation

Prisons in the 1800s were used to punish criminals so they would not re-offend on release. Prisons today try to reduce re-offending rates through education and giving prisoners work that teaches them new skills. However, they have mixed success rates, and the general public do not always support what can be portrayed as 'holiday camp' prisons.

Now try this

Jot down as many purposes of prison today as you can.

You should know about the use and purpose of prison as a punishment.

Continuity and change

This topic looks at continuity and change in crime and punishment between Roman Britain and c1450. Consider the whole period before going into the details.

Continuity

Crimes mainly stayed the same across this period.

- The most common crime was theft.
- Laws (and therefore crimes and punishments) were made by wealthy men who often protected their own interests.
- Crime prevention was low.
- The aims of punishment were deterrence and retribution (revenge).

- Punishments were cheap and quick to carry out.
- Criminals were held totally responsible for their crimes – circumstances were not taken into account.
- The law often punished women more harshly than men. Those at the top of society were treated differently from those at the bottom.

Change

Some changes during this time (see the graph below) affected punishment and law enforcement. Examples include:

- the influence of the Christian Church from Saxon times, resulting in lower use of the death penalty
- stability of the ruler, meant better law enforcement and therefore less crime
- new rulers (especially foreign conquerors) who used harsh punishments to deter rebellions.

Key events

Two major events had a great impact on society, and therefore on crime and punishment, during this period: the Romans leaving Britain in the 5th century and the Norman conquest in 1066.

EXAM ALERT!

Make sure you are clear about the situation in the Roman, Saxon and Norman period. Know what order they were in, what changed and what stayed the same.

Students have struggled with this topic in recent exams – **be prepared!**

Results Plus

Patterns of change

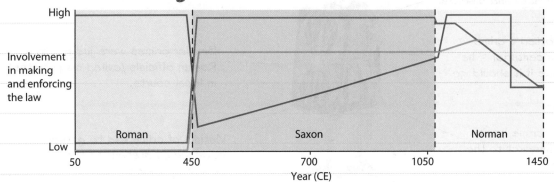

Now try this

Give **three** reasons why levels of punishment changed from Roman times to c1450.

Roman Britain

Roman Britain had a clear system for dealing with crime. You need to be familiar with this approach.

Roman society

Roman society was hierarchical, patriarchal and unequal.

Hierarchical
The wealthy at the top and slaves at the bottom.

Patriarchal
Women, children and slaves obeyed male head of the family.

Unequal
Poverty led to crime. The wealthy had all the power.

Roman law

Roman society may seem different from modern-day Britain, but their laws are familiar.

✓ The parts of Britain ruled by Rome had one central system of law and law enforcement.

✓ Laws were written down and displayed so people knew them.

✓ Suspects were considered innocent until proven guilty in a fair trial in a court where evidence had been presented.

Types of crime

Most crimes were **against property** (petty theft, selling underweight goods and burglary). Crimes **against the person** (street violence and murder) were rare. Crimes **against authority** (plotting against the emperor or refusing to conform to the official state religion) received the harshest punishments. People were punished according to whether they were men, women, citizens, non-citizens or slaves.

Punishments

The death penalty was used often under Roman rule. Punishments included:
• flogging and beating
• repaying the cost of stolen goods
• cutting off limbs
• being sent into exile
• being forced to become a gladiator
• execution by various methods, including crucifixion or being thrown to the lions.

Law enforcement

Roman legions were in charge of dealing with riots and disorder.

People reported a crime to the local centurion – he would decide if it should go to court.

Victims of crime had to take the suspect to the centurion.

Very serious crimes were tried by the Roman Governor of Britain.

Smaller crimes were judged by Roman officials (called magistrates) in local courts.

Victims of crime had to gather evidence to present to the centurion, then the court.

Now try this

Give **three** examples of how Roman society influenced crime and punishment.

Anglo-Saxon England

When the Romans left in the 5th century, the unified system of law largely collapsed. Britain was conquered by tribes from Germany – Angles, Saxons and Jutes – who formed different kingdoms with different systems of law.

Law enforcement

In the Saxon period, crime victims or their relatives could directly punish the criminal or their family. This could lead to blood feuds. Wergeld payments were increasingly used as an alternative.

By the year 1000, tithings were used to give people joint responsibility for crime and punishment.

- Anyone who witnessed a crime had to raise a 'hue and cry' by shouting to alert others and chasing the criminal.

- Guilt or innocence was decided in a court by a jury of local free men. If the jury couldn't decide, the accused was handed over to the Church for trial by ordeal (hot water, cold water or fire).

Blood feuds were when murder was avenged by a relative who killed someone in the killer's family. That death would then also be avenged. So these feuds could last for generations.

Wergeld was a payment made to the family of the murdered person. Different prices were paid depending on the importance of the victim. The system reduced violence and improved community relations.

Tithings were a collection of ten free men. If one was accused of a crime, the others made sure he went to court or they had to pay a fine for him.

Punishments

Those found guilty in an Anglo-Saxon court were given one of these punishments:

- fines and compensation (the most common punishment)
- floggings and beatings
- confiscation of property
- cutting off hands, feet or tongue
- execution (rarely used).

The Church

After the Synod of Whitby in 663, most Anglo-Saxon kings were Christian and the Church began to have a big impact on crime and punishment.

- The Church created new laws, which criminalised some actions and so created new crimes such as breaking Church rules during Lent.

- The Church preferred punishments that gave 'sinners' a chance to repent.

- According to the Church, innocence or guilt could be decided by God in trial by ordeal.

Anglo-Saxon kings

Each kingdom was ruled by a king who was in overall charge of the law. Some later Anglo-Saxon kings drew up codes of law. Most law was based on custom and not written down. The power of the kings increased, especially in later years as England became more unified.

Now try this

Give **three** examples of how Anglo-Saxon crime and punishment was **(a)** similar, and **(b)** different from crime and punishment in Roman Britain.

Norman England

After the Norman conquest in 1066, England had fairly unified laws. You will need to learn about the changes during the Norman period.

Power of the king

King William kept Anglo-Saxon laws and added a few more of his own. As a result, his power increased and he had far greater authority than the Anglo-Saxon kings.

Law enforcement

Anglo-Saxon systems of tithings, the hue and cry and the court system continued, with the addition of trial by combat. However, more county courts were set up for serious crimes.

About 30% of England (including farms and villages) became 'Royal Forest'.

These areas were protected by new Forest Laws.

It was a crime to kill animals like deer or cut down trees without permission.

A large network of officials policed the laws of the forest.

Punishments for breaking laws of the forest were very harsh.

Fines and forest taxes added to the king's wealth and power.

Norman Forest Law

The Church

The Church increased its influence over the law after the Norman invasion.

- 'Immoral' actions (such as sex outside marriage) became crimes.
- Church courts were set up to deal with these, and for anyone not following Church rites.
- All clergy could be tried in a Church court and proved their right to this by reading a passage from the Bible. Church courts could not impose the death penalty, so some people learned a Bible passage off by heart to claim 'benefit of clergy'.
- Nobody could be arrested if they were in a church (right of sanctuary). If they confessed their crime, they would be allowed to leave the country.

Punishment

The Norman invasion was not welcomed by the Anglo-Saxons and there was much resistance for the first few years. Harsh punishments carried out publicly were seen as the best way to make people behave.

- Use of the death penalty rose dramatically, as did mutilations and amputations.
- The death penalty was widened to cover more offences, including theft.
- Some of the worst punishments were for breaking Forest Laws.
- Paying compensation to victims of crime declined.
- Very minor crimes were still punished by fines, whipping or time in the stocks or pillory.

Now try this

What similarities are there between Norman and Anglo-Saxon crime and punishment?

It's important to revise what stayed the same as well as how much change there was from one period to another.

Later Medieval England

Law and order completely broke down during the civil war of 1135–54. After Henry II became king in 1154, he started to restore the king's power and reduce the power of nobles.

Types of crime

Petty theft was still the most common crime, and the Forest Laws still caused resentment. Crime in the Middle Ages was closely linked with economic conditions. When prices rose, so did crime.

Constitutions of Clarendon

In 1164, Henry II brought together Anglo-Saxon, Norman and royal laws. This enforced the same system throughout England, which is still the basis of our Common Law today!

Punishments

Hangings gradually decreased, but other physical punishments continued. Fines became common because many juries would not convict their neighbours unless they regularly offended. The king also pardoned some criminals. Crimes against authority were still harshly punished.

Heresy

Having religious beliefs that were different to the official religion of the state (Catholicism) was a crime against authority and punished by death (even though it was tried in a Church court).

Methods of law enforcement

Local law enforcement	Central law enforcement
The 'hue and cry' system of witnesses raising the alarm and chasing criminals continued, as did tithings.	In 1285, Edward I passed a law which allowed sheriffs to form 'posses' of local men to help chase and catch criminals.
Most villages had a manor court where the local lord acted as judge for petty crimes. Henry II encouraged the use of juries to decide guilt or innocence. This was normal by the end of the 14th century.	In 1361, the Justices of the Peace Act gave JPs power to hear minor crimes in small courts, four times a year. JPs (normally local lords) were appointed by the king. They worked on their own or with other JPs.
Trial by ordeal and by combat continued to be used by communities as informal methods of law enforcement if juries were not able to reach a verdict. They were abolished in 1215.	The most serious criminal cases (those which carried the death penalty) were tried in royal courts, either in London or by judges who travelled to each county twice a year.
All counties now had their own prisons to keep accused people before their trial by the royal judges sent out from London.	Henry II tried but failed to get rid of Church courts, which continued to try the clergy or ordinary people for moral crimes.

Now try this

List ways in which law enforcement differed in the later medieval period from the Norman period.

Witchcraft 1

Witchcraft had been a crime since medieval times but in the 16th and 17th centuries it was regarded as a more serious crime and harshly punished.

Timeline

1563 Increase of prosecutions under Elizabeth I after a new law defined minor witchcraft and major witchcraft (punishable by death)

1642–49 The English Civil War sparked the worst phase of witch-hunting hysteria

1736 All witchcraft laws were abolished

Witchcraft

1542 Henry VIII passed a new law – witchcraft became a crime against authority (punished by death)

1604 Major witch-hunts after James I enforced all other witchcraft laws

1685 The last execution in England for witchcraft

Changing attitudes – as charity for the poor declined, people were worried they might be 'cursed' by a poor person they had refused to help.

Attitudes of authority – King James I strongly believed in witchcraft and wrote a book about it (*Demonologie*, 1597). Several JPs also believed in witches.

Religion – after the Reformation, the government wanted everyone to have the same religion as the ruler. Witchcraft, therefore became a crime against authority (the state) rather than against religion.

Reputation – women who knew about herbal medicines were considered wise if successful or witches if not. Some women said they were witches to frighten others. Old women who lived alone were considered strange.

Reasons why witchcraft became a serious crime and was harshly punished

Economic problems – during the period 1580–1645, unemployment increased, wages dropped and prices rose. Some people looked for scapegoats to blame for their bad luck.

Social changes / tensions – some people were accused of witchcraft because others disliked them. A widow living alone was often resented because she often asked for help.

War – Civil conflict led people to become more suspicious of others.

Now try this

Identify examples of when there were heightened concerns about witchcraft and give reasons why.

Witchcraft 2

Attitudes to witchcraft gradually began to change. You will need to know the reasons why.

Why women?

Before the 20th century, women were often punished more harshly than men for crime. Most historians see witchcraft as part of this unequal treatment – over 90% of those accused of witchcraft were women.

- Women who were older or widowed often lived alone and tended to have knowledge of herbs which they made a living from.
- Christianity portrayed women as easily tempted by the devil and able to make men do evil things.
- According to some historians, many men feared or hated women. This hatred is called misogyny.

Evidence of witchcraft

The following were all used as evidence to convict people of witchcraft:

Unusual marks on the body of the person accused

If they did not bleed when pricked with a needle

Witness accounts

If they floated when thrown into water

Two proven witches swearing the accused was a witch too

Confessions

'Possessed' children acting as accusers

Number of deaths

People found guilty of major witchcraft were usually hanged. Many others died when communities carried out unofficial 'trials' such as the 'swimming test', so it is difficult to know how many were killed.

EXAM ALERT!

Make sure you can explain how this 'evidence' was used to convict people of witchcraft.

Students have struggled with this topic in recent exams – **be prepared!**

 ResultsPlus

The Witchfinder General

During the Civil War, Matthew Hopkins accused 36 women of witchcraft (often torturing them to confess), and 19 were hanged. Hopkins, who called himself the Witchfinder General, earned money for each witch executed.

Changing attitudes

Changes in the attitudes of the authorities can be seen in the decline of witchcraft prosecution after the Civil War. Witchcraft laws were abolished in 1736. The general public were much slower to change – unofficial witchcraft trials continued during the latter part of the 18th century.

Reasons why witchcraft stopped being a crime

Economic and social changes: greater prosperity and political stability reduced social tension.

Less superstition: although some people still believed in witches and the devil, others (especially the educated) became less superstitious.

Science: increased experimentation from 1660 began to explain things that people previously thought were the work of witches.

Now try this

Jot down reasons why witch trials declined after the Civil War.

Conscientious objection

Conscientious objectors are people who have religious, moral or political objections to war. For a short time in the 20th century, conscientious objection became a crime.

Conscription

Conscription is a law that states that everyone of a certain age who is fit and healthy has to fight in the armed forces. Anyone refusing to fight is committing a crime and could therefore be punished. Conscription has been introduced twice in Britain – during the First and Second World Wars.

Don't forget that people doing work essential to the country were exempt from conscription.

Attitudes to conscientious objectors

The punishment and treatment of conscientious objectors (COs) was very different in the two wars, showing how people in authority changed their attitude. However, the general public's attitude was similar in both world wars – they thought COs were cowards and traitors. Some were physically attacked, sacked from their jobs or found it difficult to get work.

Different treatment

First World War	Second World War
Conscription for men: from 1916.	Conscription: from April 1939 for men, from December 1941 for women.
A clause in law excused conscientious objectors.	A clause in law excused conscientious objectors.
About 16 000 men refused to fight.	Over 59 000 men and women refused to fight.
Military tribunals made up of military officers and professionals decided if CO was genuine.	Tribunals (minus military people) judged if CO was genuine.
Only 400 were given total exemption on grounds of conscience.	All except 12 204 were given complete or partial exemption.
'Alternativists' were given non-combatant roles.	Those with partial exemption were given non-combatant roles.
'Absolutists' were imprisoned, given brutal treatment and hard labour. Ten died in prison, 63 died after release and 31 had breakdowns.	A far smaller percentage of those not given exemption were sent to prison and those who did were not treated as harshly.

Alternativists

People who refused to kill or attack anyone during war, but who would take part in other ways like driving ambulances, bearing stretchers, doing factory work or farming. Some did dangerous jobs such as bomb disposal.

Absolutists

People who refused to do anything to contribute to the war because they felt that war was wrong. Of those not given exemption, all were imprisoned in the First World War but only a few were punished in the Second World War.

Now try this

List reasons why there were more conscientious objectors in the Second World War than the First World War.

Domestic violence 1

This topic examines how and why domestic violence became a criminal offence that is increasingly harshly punished.

Definitions

Today, domestic violence is classed as verbal, mental or physical abuse by the partner of someone in a relationship. This could be against men by women or within gay and lesbian relationships. However, most domestic violence incidents are the abuse of a woman by her husband or boyfriend. Although this topic focuses on male violence against women, it is important to remember that recent laws apply to both male and female victims and perpetrators.

Slow change

Before the 20th century most people accepted that a man had a right to beat his wife and children 'in moderation'.

- In the 19th century, the law stated that violence against wives was classed as assault. However, most judges only gave light punishments even for severe violence.

- The 19th century saw a growth in social condemnation of 'wife beaters' by communities and in newspapers.

- During the 19th century some women campaigned for more rights but could not vote on equal terms with men until 1928.

- In 1970 women were given equal pay. In 1975 discrimination against women became illegal.

Women were too scared to speak out and make complaints against their husbands.

Society's attitudes towards women.

Domestic violence in middle and upper class homes was 'invisible' – people rarely knew about it.

The belief that the law should not apply to private family life.

Why wasn't domestic violence a crime before 1976?

Laws were made by men.

Laws were enforced by men (most police officers and judges were male).

Domestic violence in 19th century was associated with alcohol and the working class.

Now try this

Jot down reasons why it took so long for domestic violence to be treated as a crime.

Domestic violence 2

New laws and changing attitudes brought greater attention to domestic violence.

What led to change?

Campaign groups
Women's rights groups raised public awareness and put pressure on the government to change the law. Examples include Chiswick Women's Aid set up by Erin Pizzey in 1971 and the National Women's Aid Federation set up in 1974.

New state roles
It became more acceptable for the state to interfere in 'private' lives if it needed to – for example, to protect children, give unemployed people financial support and give everyone free healthcare on the NHS.

Female political power
Since 1928 women have had equal voting rights with men and some have become politicians. It is very important for MPs to win women's votes. In 1971 Jack Ashley was the first MP to raise the issue of domestic violence in Parliament.

The media
Newspapers and news programmes reported more incidents of domestic violence and the work of campaign groups.

these led to

1976 Domestic Violence Act Victims of domestic violence could gain non-molestation and exclusion orders (which meant an abuser could not return to the home).

In 1990 the police were told to collect statistics on domestic violence separately from other cases of assault; this showed the scale of the problem.

1991 Rape within marriage became a criminal offence in England and Wales.

1996 Family Law Act gave victims more protection. Arrest became automatic where violence had been used or threatened.

The media began to include domestic violence storylines in radio and television dramas which heightened awareness.

2004 Domestic Violence, Crime and Victims Act
Male and female victims were given the same protection. The powers of the police and courts to act increased.

Law enforcement

The 1976 Domestic Violence Act was a start, but judges were reluctant to grant exclusion orders and give police the power to arrest suspects who broke orders. Things have improved since then, with further laws, and judges giving increasingly severe punishments.

Changing attitudes

As people increasingly thought of domestic violence as a crime, more pressure was put on law-makers to make it a crime. However, not everyone agreed – laws were resisted, particularly by some members of the police and some judges.

Now try this

List the factors that helped to bring about a change to the law regarding domestic violence.

Life on the Plains

Plains Indians depended on each other, the land and animals for survival.

Role of buffalo and horses

The Indians needed buffalo and horses to survive. Buffalo lived on the Plains. Horses had been introduced by Spanish invaders. The Indians bred and traded (or even stole) them.

Catching buffalo was quicker and easier on horseback.

Indians could not live on the Plains without horses because they would not survive.

Every part of a buffalo (except its heart, which was left on the plain) was used for food, clothing and equipment.

Wealth and status were measured by how many horses an Indian or tribe had.

Horses were used in war.

Horses carried the Indians and their belongings on their journey to find buffalo.

The Indians believed a buffalo's heart gave new life to a herd.

Women and children cut up the buffalo meat. It was eaten raw or cooked. Some (known as jerky) was stored for winter.

Plains Indians were nomads. They ate wild fruits and plants but did not settle long enough to grow crops.

Fighting and war

Plains Indians had very different attitudes to war from Europeans. They never fought to own land or to conquer/destroy other tribes. Bravery was about being responsible and staying alive to provide for your family, not about fighting against all odds.

Why did Indians fight?	How did they fight?
• To demonstrate skills, bravery and courage. • To protect hunting ground. • For revenge or honour. • To capture horses or weapons. • To help tribal unity. • So that chiefs could test their power and position. • So that elders could control the younger braves.	• In short raids with small groups of braves. • Warriors gained honour by 'counting coup'– this meant performing feats such as touching an enemy with a hand or stick. • Killing was rare. A few tribes scalped dead enemies so their spirits could not fight in heaven. • Retreating (to stay alive for their families) was seen as a responsible action. They would refuse to fight if they couldn't win.

Now try this

Jot down the ways Indians used buffalo. Use your list to write a paragraph explaining why buffalo were important to the Plains Indians.

Indian society

Indians lived in groups known as 'bands'. Each band had a chief and a council, and was part of a tribe.

 Bands

Most people in a band were related to each other. Bands were led by chiefs and had councils of advisers. Council members agreed everything the band did. The survival and protection of the band as a whole was seen as more important than the individuals within it.

 Chiefs and councils

Chiefs were chosen because of their wisdom and skills as warriors/hunters. They were rarely chiefs for life. Chiefs and councils decided where their bands would go and what should happen to those who broke with customs and traditions. But they did not have to be obeyed.

 Tribes

Bands in the same tribe supported each other during crises. Tribal meetings of all the bands were held each year to arrange marriages, trade horses and discuss issues. Chiefs and elders formed the tribal councils that advised tribal chiefs. Some tribes (e.g. the Sioux) were part of larger groups called nations.

 Warrior societies

The best warriors from each band formed its society. Members of the warrior societies supervised hunting and protected their bands from attack. All short raids and wars were led by the warrior society and the band's council would always consult them before they made decisions.

Tipis

Every Indian family lived in a tipi, made of wooden poles and buffalo skins.

- Tipis were cone shaped, to protect against strong winds.
- Tipis could easily be taken down, so were ideal for life on the move. A collapsed tipi could form a travois and be pulled by a horse.
- The bottom was rolled up in summer to let air in and was banked with earth in winter to keep the inside warm.

Family roles

A band saw every member as being equally important to its survival.

- Men (braves) hunted and fought enemies. Women (squaws) made clothing, fed the family and looked after their tipi.
- Everyone looked after children, who were taught the skills of their parents.
- Elders were respected for their wisdom but were left behind to die if they threatened the survival of a band.

EXAM ALERT!

As well as describing Indian culture, you need to be able to explain how it helped them live on the Plains.

Students have struggled with this topic in recent exams – **be prepared!**   ResultsPlus

Now try this

List **three** examples to illustrate the prioritisation of the band over individuals.

 The band, as a group, was seen as more important than its individuals. This is a key point to understand.

Why move west?

You need to know the reasons why people travelled and moved west.

Mountain men

These were the first white people to cross the Great Plains and Rocky Mountains.

- They trapped animals for fur, which they traded at stations known as 'forts'.
- They worked with (and sometimes fought) Indians. Many had Indian wives.
- They guided others along the routes they found.
- They helped government explorers by drawing maps and giving tips.

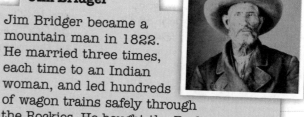

Jim Bridger

Jim Bridger became a mountain man in 1822. He married three times, each time to an Indian woman, and led hundreds of wagon trains safely through the Rockies. He bought the Rocky Mountain Fur company in 1830, and when the fur trade collapsed he set up Fort Bridger, a trading post that provided supplies to migrants on the Oregon Trail.

Push and pull factors for moving west

Pull factors

👍 Freedom and independence
👍 Fertile land
👍 Space
👍 Furs and fish
👍 Gold

Push factors

👎 Collapse of wheat prices
👎 Overpopulation
👎 Persecution
👎 Unemployment

Timeline

Moving west

1837 Bank crash causes economic depression: people lose savings, wages are cut and unemployment increases
Wheat prices fall; many Midwest **farmers** face ruin

1842 Government act makes cheap land available in Oregon

1848 Gold is discovered in California

1874 Gold is discovered in the Black Hills (Dakota)

1820s + 30s
Mountain men bring news of fertile land, furs and fish on the other side of the Rockies

1840 Population of Missouri reaches 353 000 (from 14 000 in 1830)

1846 Governor of Illinois tells **Mormons** to leave

1858–59 Gold is discovered in the Rockies

Now try this

Give reasons why these people may have decided to move west: farmers, Mormons, unemployed workers, failed businessmen.

The reasons why different people moved west is key to understanding the American West so make sure you revise them all.

The journey west

The journey west began at Independence, Missouri. Here, wagon trains (usually made up of 20 wagons or more) gathered for the trip, which took eight to nine months.

First successful wagons arrived in Oregon in 1843 and California in 1844.

Between 1840 and 1860, around 34 000 people died on the journey west.

Crossing the Great Plains was made dangerous by: sandstorms, quicksand, extreme heat, storms, disease, stampeding buffalo, hostile Indians and a lack of supplies.

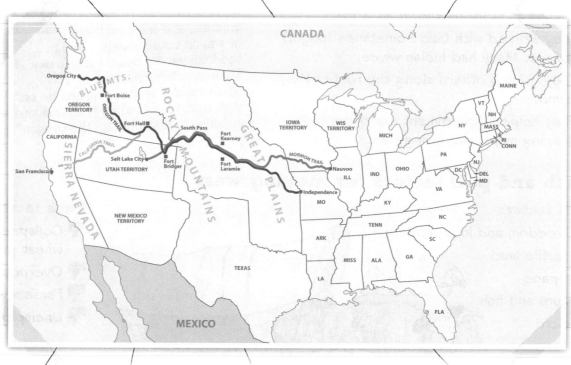

Prairie grass was good for animals at the right time of year.

The wagon trains usually began in April or May.

Early migrants used mountain men or Indians as guides; later ones relied on pamphlets.

Each trail crossed two mountain ranges: the Rockies, and either the Blue Mountains or the Sierra Nevada. They were steep, there was little to hunt, and the weather could be bad. Wagons were hauled across using chains, ropes and pulleys. Injuries were common.

The Donner Party

The Donner Party, led by Jacob and George Donner, left Missouri for California in May 1846 with 60 wagons and 300 people.

* This wagon train was well equipped but had more women, elderly people and children than normal.

* At Fort Bridger, a smaller group of about 80 people tried to take a 'short cut' (they were using a leaflet for guidance).

* Four wagons broke, 300 cattle died and one man killed another.

* They arrived late in Sierra Nevada and were trapped by heavy snow.

* A group, sent for help, took 32 days to reach Johnston's Ranch.

* To survive, both groups ate their dead. Rescue parties found them in January 1847.

A 19th century engraving of the stranded Donner Party

Now try this

Make a table of the dangers migrants could face on the journey west and how they could prepare for each one.

The Gold Rush

Gold was found in California in 1848. Many migrants were attracted to the benefits this discovery could offer them.

	Who were they?	Where did they live and what were these places like?
Surface gold miners (e.g. the forty-niners)	• Men without families from different backgrounds (including Europe and eastern US states) who planned to go home when they were rich. • They panned for gold in rivers, digging down a few metres to look for it. • Few succeeded in their dreams of wealth.	• They set up shanty towns of tents and small cabins. Disease (dysentery, typhoid, scurvy) was common. • Saloons emerged where miners drank alcohol, gambled and found prostitutes. • Violence and crime were high. Claim-jumping was common and often led to murder. • There were no formal state laws, so miners formed their own courts for crime. But these were often corrupt and unjust.
Professional miners	• Men with experience of deep underground mining (where most gold was). They arrived in the mid-1850s and wanted to settle, so they brought their families and possessions with them. • They were backed by businessmen in the eastern states and made gold mining a rich industry.	• They built permanent and cleaner homes, so proper towns started to grow. • Law and order was formalised: claims were recorded; sheriffs appointed to arrest criminals; and courts set up. • Trials were quick and punishment (flogging, banishment, hanging) harsh. Justice was rarely fair. • Vigilante groups held instant trials and immediately hanged those found guilty. People grew to fear vigilantes more than criminals.

Impact of the Gold Rush

The Gold Rush stimulated movement of people and money west in the 1850s, made California rich, made San Francisco an important port and financial centre, resulted in a new railroad from east to west and made the USA a world leader in trade. However, the native Indians of California were virtually wiped out, and racial conflict caused workers from China and Mexico (for example) to suffer at the hands of white Americans.

EXAM ALERT!

Make sure you know the difference between the gold rushes of 1849, 1859 and 1874.

Students have struggled with this topic in recent exams – **be prepared!**   Results**Plus**

Now try this

List at least **three** differences between gold migrants and other types of migrant.

The Gold Rush was an important event so make sure you know how it was similar and how it was different to other migrations.

The Mormons

The Mormons were religious people who settled in Utah, initially around Salt Lake City.

Joseph Smith

Smith founded the Church of Latter-Day Saints – his followers are known as Mormons. His persuasive public speaking meant numbers grew to several hundred by 1830. He taught Mormons to obey him because he said his decisions were inspired by God. He was murdered in Illinois, 1845.

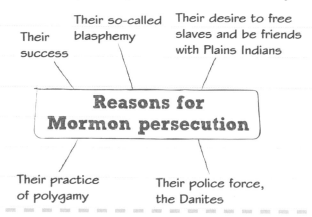

Reasons for Mormon persecution

- Their success
- Their so-called blasphemy
- Their desire to free slaves and be friends with Plains Indians
- Their practice of polygamy
- Their police force, the Danites

Moving from state to state

New York State (1823–31) → Ohio (1831–37) → Missouri (1837–38) → Illinois (1838–46) → Utah (1847–present)

Journey to the Great Salt Lake

When Smith died in 1845, Brigham Young became leader. The Mormons' persecution in Illinois forced him and 1500 others to find land that no one else wanted – near the Great Salt Lake. To make the journey, he:

- split everyone into groups, each with a leader
- gave everyone a specific role
- taught them how to form their wagons into a circle for safety
- insisted on discipline and regular rest.

His was the first of many Mormon wagon trains to make the 2250 km journey.

A Mormon state?

Utah first belonged to Mexico. It became a US territory in 1848, with Young its first governor. Mormons ignored some laws made in Washington. This annoyed non-Mormon settlers, but the Danites crushed their opposition. In 1857, a non-Mormon governor and 1500 federal soldiers arrived. Non-Mormons were killed (Mormons blamed Indians, non-Mormons blamed Danites) and tensions rose. Utah was finally allowed to become a state in 1890 as long as the governor wasn't a Mormon and polygamy was banned.

Why were the Mormons successful in Utah?

Their religious faith encouraged them to work very hard and prevented them giving up in the face of terrible hardship.

Brigham Young was in control and made good decisions.

The Mormon Church owned all land, water and timber, which were allocated to families. Towns ran efficiently.

Salt Lake City

They dug irrigation ditches which meant farm land had enough water.

A Perpetual Emigration Fund allowed thousands of Mormons to emigrate to Utah.

Young attracted settlers with varying skills and occupations to live in the new towns he founded.

Now try this

Jot down reasons for the Mormons' successful settling in Utah. Which reason was most important?

Settling the Plains

You need to be able to explain why white Americans were encouraged to move onto the Plains.

Why settle the Plains?

Security

In 1783, the USA had 13 states. By 1853, wars, treaties and money meant its borders had expanded to most of modern-day America. However, the government worried that Mexico, France and Great Britain, who had owned the land, would want it back. So the government filled it with loyal white Americans to fight enemies and increase prosperity.

Manifest Destiny

For a long time, many white Americans thought it was their 'Manifest Destiny' to live across the whole of America. The concept was spread by the government who commissioned pictures promoting the idea to people.

American Progress by John Gast. This is a visual representation of the belief in Manifest Destiny.

How did the government help settle the Plains?

Selling land
- The government sold off Public Domain Land, which anyone had been allowed to live on.
- It was divided into 10 km² 'townships', then 640-acre plots which sold for $1 per acre.
- Ordinary people couldn't afford these plots, so speculators bought, then sold, them for a profit.

Railroads
The government gave land on either side of new railroad tracks to the railroad companies. This encouraged them to expand the tracks across the Plains. The first Great Plains railroad was finished in 1869.

Homestead Act 1862
- Speculators were barred, so that ordinary people could live on the Plains.
- Settlers could officially claim 160 acres to live on and farm.
- After five years, settlers (known as 'homesteaders') were sold a certificate of ownership for $30.

Growth of towns
Railroads meant that people and freight could reach the Plains. Railroad companies sold much of the 155 million acres they owned to help new Plains towns grow.

Now try this

Give reasons why the US government wanted white Americans to live on the Great Plains.

Farming the Plains

Life on the Plains often meant overcoming different types of problems.

Problems	Explanation	Solutions
Lack of timber (not many trees on the Plains)	There was nothing to build houses with.	People built sod houses made from blocks of earth.
	There was nothing to make fences to contain cattle and protect crops from buffalo.	In 1874, Joseph Glidden invented barbed wire, which was quick and cheap to erect.
	There was nothing to use for cooking and heating.	Women collected buffalo and cattle dung, which was used for fuel.
Lack of water (not enough to store)	There was low rainfall and few rivers and lakes.	Drills were developed to find underground water, then wind pumps built to bring it to the surface.
Hard, arid land (crops wouldn't grow)	Ploughs often broke going through deep-rooted grass.	Mass-produced and stronger machinery from eastern factories helped cultivate land more easily.
	Low rainfall prevented growth of crops like maize and wheat, which farmers were used to growing.	New techniques like dry farming (which conserved rainfall) were used. Migrants from Russia brought Turkey Red wheat, which thrived on the Plains.
Natural disasters (prairie fires and pests destroyed crops and land)	Pests such as grasshoppers could destroy a whole season's crop. Fire spread quickly and burned everything.	There were no solutions. Homesteaders could be bankrupted by such disasters.
Land holdings were too small	The 160 acres allocated in the Homestead Act could not support the average family.	The Timber and Culture Act 1873 let homesteaders have another 160 acres if they promised to plant trees on half of it. The Desert Land Act 1877 let settlers buy 640 acres of desert land cheaply.
Disease and lack of medical care (people were often ill)	Sod houses were hard to keep clean and had no sanitation.	Women cared for the sick, using their own remedies. As communities grew, doctors arrived.
Lack of education	Most homesteads were too far from towns with schools.	Women taught the young. As communities grew, single female teachers arrived and schools developed.
Isolation	Life was lonely and tough on the Plains.	Railroads improved travel and brought much-needed supplies to homesteaders. Communities worked together to build schools and churches. Women homesteaders formed valuable social networks.

Now try this

List all the ways in which women helped successfully settle the Great Plains.

It is important that you understand the role of women on the Great Plains.

The importance of railroads

Between 1860 and 1890, more than 300 000 km of railroad track was laid across the USA. You need to know why this was done and the problems faced.

Railroads would enable troops to be moved around to control Indian uprisings.

Railroads would allow all Americans to keep in touch, creating national unity.

Railroads would help to fulfil white Americans' Manifest Destiny by making it easier to migrate and secure more areas of the country.

Why did the US government need railroads to connect the east and west coasts?

Railroads would let federal law officers reach new settlements that were having problems with law and order.

Railroads would transport goods to ports in Oregon and California, which were well positioned to trade with the Far East.

Government action

Pacific Railways Act 1862
This set up the Union Pacific Railroad Company to lay track east to west, and the Central Pacific Railroad Company to lay track west to east.

Township land parcels
These were given to railroad companies next to the tracks to help finance railroad building.

Railroad companies

Laying track across the USA would be very expensive.

Railway companies could sell the land next to the track to raise more money or use it as security for borrowing money.

Problems of construction

Raising money for construction

Difficult terrain including mountains and deserts

Hostile Indians attacking railroad workers

Finding enough people to work

Dreadful living and working conditions for people building the tracks

Solutions

 Largely solved by the government's gift of free land

 Solved by great engineers and the extreme hard work of the labourers

 Remained a problem throughout the process

 Used immigrant labour from China and Ireland

Terrible weather, difficulties getting food to workers and extremely hard work remained a problem – labourers died in their hundreds

Now try this

Give reasons why the railroad companies wanted to build railroads across the whole USA.

The impact of railroads

Railroads carried people, goods and supplies all over the country. White settlers benefitted, but Plains Indians lost out.

Benefits of railroads

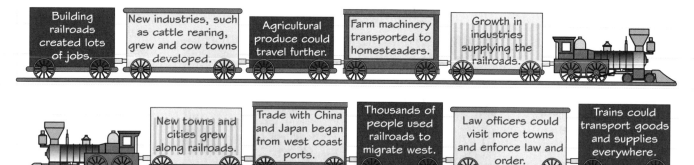

Building railroads created lots of jobs.

New industries, such as cattle rearing, grew and cow towns developed.

Agricultural produce could travel further.

Farm machinery transported to homesteaders.

Growth in industries supplying the railroads.

New towns and cities grew along railroads.

Trade with China and Japan began from west coast ports.

Thousands of people used railroads to migrate west.

Law officers could visit more towns and enforce law and order.

Trains could transport goods and supplies everywhere.

Impact on Plains Indians

The railroads created a number of disadvantages for Plains Indians.

👎 They brought in homesteaders (settlers), goods and machinery, which meant crops were sown and houses built where Indians used to roam. This land was fenced so Indians and buffalo could no longer roam across it.

👎 Plains Indians depended on buffalo, which were no longer easy to hunt with fences and homesteads in the way. Also, the railroads brought white hunters who killed buffalo for sport.

👎 Railroads criss-crossed the Plains, stopping Indians and buffalo roaming freely.

👎 Indians believed that the railroads and settlers were working against nature and ruining sacred land. The Indians had often been on good terms with white Americans before the railroads; but now they became hostile, attacking those building them. This provoked white men to become hostile towards them in turn.

A turning point?

Many historians see the construction of the railroads as a turning point in developing the West because railroads:

- helped start the USA's industrial revolution by creating increased demand for materials to build the railway and stimulating economic growth by improving access to goods and markets
- improved communications and therefore helped ease the sense of isolation felt by settlers and create communities, as well as improving national cohesion
- led to more people successfully settling in the West, as railroads made it easier to supply the goods and services people needed, and by improving law and order
- played a large role in destroying the Plains Indians' way of life.

A railroad

Now try this

Jot down the ways in which homesteaders living on the Plains benefitted from the railroads.

Make sure you understand these benefits.

Cattle trails

Cattle trails first began in 1845 when Texas joined the USA. After the Civil War they increased because more people in the cities could afford to eat beef.

Cattle trails

- White American Texans drove herds of longhorn cattle (left behind by Mexicans) to markets in New Orleans, California and Chicago.
- When they returned from the Civil War (1861–65), they found huge herds of cattle running wild.
- They drove them to northern and eastern cities where beef was worth ten times more than in Texas.
- Railroads shortened the journey. Cattle were driven to railheads and finished their journey on trains.

Charles Goodnight

Goodnight, a Texan, returned from the Civil War to find his herd of cattle had increased. He teamed up with Oliver Loving, an experienced cattle drover. Together, they established the Goodnight-Loving Trail to supply meat to the army and Indian reservations.

Problems with cattle trails

- Rustlers and Indians could steal the cattle being driven.
- Grass on some trails was poor, so the cattle arrived in bad condition.
- Some trails had little access to water.
- The cattle could stampede and be hard to control on the trail.
- The cattle trails offered no protection from the dangerous wildlife such as wolves, scorpions and snakes.
- Crossing rivers could be dangerous.
- Quicksand could sink humans and animals in minutes.
- Armed mobs might try to stop cattle crossing their land in case the cattle on the trail had a deadly tick which could infect their own cattle.
- Watching for dangers day and night was exhausting.

Joseph McCoy and Abilene

Joseph McCoy had the idea of cattle dealing at railheads in the west, rather than in the cities where the beef would be consumed. This meant buyers and sellers would meet on neutral ground, undisturbed by mobs, rustlers or Indians. McCoy built Abilene, the first cow town, and became very rich from taking a commission on every head of cattle sold in his town.

Cow towns

As the cattle industry grew and railroads moved westwards, cow towns appeared at railheads where cattle were bought and sold. Cow towns like Abilene, Dodge City and Newton had plenty of water and grass for cattle. They were most successful between 1867–85 when beef prices were at their highest. Cattle dealers, cowboys and saloon and hotel owners all made money.

Now try this

Jot down **three** reasons why the cattle industry began to boom after 1865.

Cattle ranches

Permanent ranches had a number of advantages over cattle trails.

Jon Iliff

Iliff decided to graze cattle instead of driving them from Texas, so his was the first large ranch on the Plains. His breeding experiments produced better tasting meat. Railroad workers and Sioux Indians bought his beef. New refrigerated railroad cars meant he could slaughter cattle before transporting them.

The benefits

Permanent ranches meant that cattle survived longer and grew fatter than on trails. After the Fort Laramie Treaty (1851), cowboys had to pay Indians to drive cattle across their land. Ranching generally avoided clashes with Indians and homesteaders, as there was no need for cowboys to cross their land.

What were ranches like?

The first ranches on the Great Plains were 'open range' – ranchers claimed rights to land and water but didn't own anything. At the centre were bunkhouses for cowboys, stables for horses and barns for storage. Land was unfenced and cattle roamed freely, so every cow was branded to show who it belonged to. The peak of the beef industry was between 1880 and 1885.

What led to the cattle bust?

Too many cattle
As cattlemen made more money, they bought and bred more cattle.

Overgrazing
There was too little grass, especially in the 1883 drought.

Prices dropped
An oversupply of beef meant prices dropped.

Less profit
Lower prices meant less profit. Some cattlemen sold up, others became bankrupt.

Winter of 1886
Temperatures dropped as low as −55°C and at least 15 per cent of cattle and many cowboys died. More cattlemen went bankrupt.

New ranches

After the bust, ranches had to change.
• They were smaller fenced-in areas producing fewer but better quality cattle.
• They were less dependent on the weather as small herds could be brought closer to buildings for shelter.
• They were more sustainable, as fewer cattle needed less grass and water.

Now try this

Write a **brief** summary of what Charles Goodnight, Joseph McCoy and John Iliff did.

Make sure you are familiar with all these key people.

Cowboys

Cowboys were often tough loners who worked hard and had a wild lifestyle.

What they wore

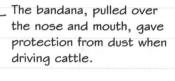

The hat (Stetson) gave protection from the sun, rain and cold.

The bandana, pulled over the nose and mouth, gave protection from dust when driving cattle.

A saddle was a cowboy's most important possession.

A lariat or lasso was used to catch cattle.

High-heeled boots meant their feet couldn't slip through stirrups.

Chaps protected cowboys' legs from vegetation and the weather.

Spurs were worn at all times.

Who were they?

Cowboys were mostly young single men. They were black American, Indian, Spanish and Mexican as well as white American. Many were former soldiers or drifters. Some were criminals on the run.

What were they like?

Cowboys were tough, hard-working and hard-drinking. On long trails they could ride for between 12 and 24 hours a day in all weathers. Cowboys on the same cattle drive often worked miles apart, so life could be lonely.

A changing role

Cowboys on trails	Cowboys on ranches
Work was seasonal, from spring round-up to the long drive in the autumn.	Work was year-round and full-time, but fewer were needed.
Work included rounding up, branding and driving cattle hundreds of miles. They also looked out for sick and injured cattle. They started fast, then slowed to about 20 km a day for grazing.	Work included rounding up, branding and driving to market, but over much smaller distances. They also checked ranch boundaries, mended fences and looked out for sick and injured cattle.
Dangers included stampeding cattle, wild animals, crossing rivers and quicksand, rustlers, hostile Indians and extreme weather.	Dangers were fewer than on trails, but wild animals and Indian attacks were still threats.
They slept in the open air and cooked on campfires.	They slept in bunkhouses and used cookhouses.
In their free time, cowboys might visit saloons and brothels in cow towns.	Drinking, gambling, guns and knives were banned. Many struggled to adapt to this lifestyle.

Now try this

List reasons why the work of cowboys changed between 1865 and 1895?

Law and order 1

Mining and cow towns sprang up very quickly without any law enforcers. Those who lived there thought they should sort out their own problems.

Why so violent?

Most people carried guns and few respected the law. Law enforcers (like sheriffs) had to travel long distances to these towns, and were often criminals themselves. There was lots of conflict between ethnic groups (Europeans, black and white Americans, Chinese, Indians) living on the same land because of differing ambitions. Many former Civil War soldiers went west and found civilian life difficult.

Crime

Here are some common crimes in mining and cow towns.

- (X) Bank robbery
- (X) Horse stealing
- (X) Cattle rustling
- (X) Racial attacks
- (X) Claim jumping
- (X) Trail or train robbery
- (X) Fence cutting
- (X) Murder

Dodge City

Cowboys often let off steam in cow towns. Dodge City, for example, had a terrible reputation for gambling, womanising and shoot-outs. However, although there was violence and lawlessness, their reputations were often not fully deserved.

Famous lawbreakers

Belle Starr

Belle Starr planned and carried out robberies. She went to prison for horse theft and was shot dead in 1889.

Jesse James

James was one of the 'Quantrill raiders' during the Civil War – attacking and murdering individuals and terrorising 'anti-Confederate' communities. In 1863, the raiders killed 150 people and set fire to 180 buildings in Lawrence. After the war, his new gang robbed banks and trains, and killed people. When they robbed a Minnesota bank, the town fought back. Only James and brother Frank escaped. He changed his name and started a new gang – but one of his fellow criminals (Robert Ford) killed him and was given a reward.

Billy the Kid

Billy the Kid began stealing cattle in Arizona. In 1877 he was arrested for murder but escaped. His employer, John Tunstall, was murdered and Billy joined 'the regulators' gang who killed many men, including Sheriff Brady, in revenge. Kid was arrested for murdering Sheriff Brady even though there was an amnesty. He then escaped twice more! Eventually, he was caught and killed in a shoot-out by Sheriff Pat Garrett. He was 22 years old.

(Now try this)

Give **three** reasons why cow towns such as Dodge City had reputations for being lawless.

Law and order 2

Maintaining law and order was sometimes undertaken legally and sometimes undertaken by groups working outside the law.

Vigilante committees (outside law)

People joined vigilante committees, usually run by community leaders. These groups caught criminals, held instant trials and lynched (hanged) culprits or ran them out of town.

Private agencies

Non-government agencies like the Texas Rangers worked within the law. Banks, railroad and stagecoach companies used agencies to find criminals and bring them to justice.

Legal law enforcement

In the 1860s, most areas in the West were territories, not states. This meant the federal government in Washington DC was responsible for law and order.

Federal government appointed

US marshals and deputy marshals who were responsible for law and order in a state or territory.	Federal judges who toured a large area and held trials for those arrested.

Towns appointed local people to maintain law and order

Sheriffs (appointed for two years)	Marshals (appointed for one year)

In territories, there were so few judges that justice could take months, so local vigilantes would try to resolve matters. By contrast, states could appoint their own judges to try state lawbreakers.

William Tilghman

Tilghman gained a reputation as an honest lawman. He pursued criminals but rarely killed them. He became Deputy Marshal of Oklahoma and, with Heck Thomas and Chris Madsen, helped to wipe out organised crime.

Wyatt Earp

Earp was a law enforcer who lost his job several times for breaking the law. He and his brothers 'ruled' Tombstone in Arizona until a gunfight, which they won against impossible odds. The judge (a relative) decided they were not guilty of murder, but they lost their control of Tombstone. Wyatt left and resorted to petty theft.

The Johnson County War, 1892

This is an example of a conflict between rival groups – the Wyoming Stock Growers Association and cattle rustlers. The WSGA was formed by large cattle ranchers. In the mid-1880s many ranchers went bankrupt, so homesteaders moved in and fenced the land.

- The WSGA said homesteaders were cattle rustling.
- Albert Bothwell and friends lynched storeowners for rustling his cattle. More violence followed.
- The WSGA hired gunmen to capture the town of Buffalo.
- They invaded in April 1892, but the Sheriff knew about the attack, so held them off until US Cavalry arrived. The attackers were tried but never convicted.

Now try this

List ways in which the federal government tried to bring law and order to the West.

Permanent Indian Frontier

The Bureau for Indian Affairs, established in 1832, decided that the Great Plains should be a reservation for all Indian tribes where they could freely roam and hunt.

Permanent Indian Frontier

The 95th meridian became the 'Permanent Indian Frontier' and by 1840, all tribes had been moved to the west of this line. However, this settlement soon came under threat.

1 Wagon trails
From the 1840s, Americans increasingly migrated west using wagon trails that crossed Indian territory. Some Indians attacked those on trails.

2 First treaties, 1849
US government treaties with the Comanche and Kiowa promised Indians land if they did not attack travellers on the Santa Fe trail.

3 Fort Laramie Treaty, 1851
This ended the Permanent Indian Frontier and moved towards concentrating Indians in certain areas.
- The government gave land in the Rocky Mountain foothills to the Cheyenne and Arapaho promising protection and payment of $50 000 a year for 10 years.
- The Cheyenne and Arapaho agreed to stop attacking Oregon Trail travellers and to allow roads and military forts to be built.

4 Gold in the Rockies, 1859
When gold was discovered on Indian land, thousands of white men moved in and railroad companies started building. This broke the Fort Laramie Treaty.

5 Cheyenne and Arapaho retaliate
Indians responded by also breaking the treaty. They attacked travellers and railroad surveyors on their land.

6 Fort Wise Treaty, 1861
This treaty, forced on chiefs, removed the land given in the Fort Laramie Treaty. It set up a smaller reservation between the Arkansas River and Sand Creek in Colorado.

7 On the warpath!
Indian warriors refused to accept the Fort Wise Treaty. They went on the warpath, raiding white settlements and attacking mail coaches.

Map:
CANADA
MONTANA
Missouri River
Blackfoot
Yellowstone River
NORTH DAKOTA
Crow
Powder River
Sioux
WYOMING
SOUTH DAKOTA
Land given up by Sioux 1858
MINNESOTA
Land given up by Cheyenne & Arapaho 1861
North Platte River
Land given up by Pawnee 1851
IOWA
COLORADO
NEBRASKA
Mississippi River
Sand Creek
KANSAS
Arkansas River
MISSOURI
Land given up by Comanche & Kiowa
NEW MEXICO
ARKANSAS
Cherokee
Chicksaw
Chocktaw
Land given up by Comanche & Kiowa 1865
Creek
Rio Grande
TEXAS
Seminole
LOUISIANA
MEXICO
Gulf of Mexico
0   500 km

Key
— Permanent Indian Frontier
← Route of Indian removal 1825–40
　Indian territory
　Mountains

Now try this

Give **three** reasons why the Permanent Indian Frontier wasn't very permanent.

The Indian Wars

Indians' ideas about warfare were very different from those of white Americans, so 'The Indian Wars' is a misleading title. You should remember this when revising the topic.

 Little Crow's War, 1862

Little Crow, a chief of the Santee Sioux Indians, lived on their reservation in Minnesota. In 1861, crops failed and food promised by the government didn't arrive – they faced starvation. In August 1862, Little Crow and others attacked the agency that ran the reservation. They stole food to share, then burned the agency buildings. They also killed several US soldiers. By October, most Santee had surrendered or been captured. They were then moved to a smaller reservation, Crow Creek. Its barren landscape caused many deaths that winter.

 The Sand Creek Massacre, 1864

The Cheyenne on the Sand Creek reservation were starving after crop failures. Led by their chief, Black Kettle, they attacked wagon trains and stole food but didn't harm travellers. After three years of attacks, Black Kettle negotiated with government officials and the army. On 29 November 1864, Colonel Chivington led a dawn raid on their camp. More than 150 Indians were massacred even though they waved white flags. Some, including Black Kettle, escaped and told other tribes what had happened. A US Senate Committee of Enquiry condemned Chivington. Both white men and Indians were horrified.

 Red Cloud's War, 1865–68

Miner John Bozeman established the Bozeman Trail, connecting the Oregon Trail to gold in Montana. Bozeman's trail broke the Fort Laramie Treaty of 1851 because it crossed the hunting grounds of the Sioux. Red Cloud (a chief of the Lakota Sioux) led attacks on the trail travellers. In 1866, the government talked with him but he stormed out when he learned that two more forts were planned along the trail. In December 1866, Captain William Fetterman and 80 soldiers rode into a trap and were massacred by the Sioux, who blocked the route so no traveller could use it. The US army then negotiated a second Fort Laramie Treaty.

Red Cloud

The Fort Laramie Treaty, 1868
- US government agrees to abandon three forts and the Bozeman Trail.
- Red Cloud agrees to move his tribe to a reservation stretching from the Black Hills of Dakota to the Missouri River.
- Both parties are in favour of the treaty. However, the Indians, now split into reservations on separate sites, find it hard to act together.

Red Cloud was successful because he joined with other Sioux tribes led by Sitting Bull and Crazy Horse, plus some Arapaho and Cheyenne tribes. He managed to keep fighting through winter (not their custom).

Now try this

List the reasons for the Indians starting conflict in:
(a) Little Crow's War. (b) The Sand Creek Massacre. (c) Red Cloud's War.

The Great Sioux War

Events of the Great Sioux War

In the 1868 Fort Laramie Treaty, the Sioux were given a large reservation in South Dakota and could roam freely in the Black Hills (sacred for the Cheyenne, Arapaho and Sioux). Whites were not allowed to settle there or prospect for gold.

As the Northern Pacific Railroad got closer to Sioux land, General George Custer led cavalrymen to protect railroad builders and look for gold. He found it!

Prospectors staked their claim to the land. The US government offered the Sioux $6 million for the Black Hills or $400 000 a year for mineral rights. They refused both offers and many bands left the Sioux reservation.

In December 1875, the Sioux were given 60 days to return to their reservation or be attacked. It was deep snow and impossible to travel.

By spring, over 7000 Indians were ready for war.

Sitting Bull, Crazy Horse and their people defeated General Crook at Rosebud River on 17 June 1876. Then they travelled west towards Little Big Horn River.

On 25 June 1876, Custer attacked the Indian camp at Little Big Horn. They were badly defeated – 225 men died and many were stripped, disfigured and scalped.

Custer's role

Some blame Custer for the army's defeat at the Battle of Little Big Horn because:
- He should have waited for back-up (but if the Indians had spotted them he might have had no choice but to attack).
- He only had 600 men and split them to try and surround the enemy – this actually meant it was easier for the much greater Indian forces to attack them.

A change in attitude?

The massacre of General Custer and his men shocked and appalled most white Americans.
- Beforehand, public opinion favoured trying to reach agreement with the Indians.
- Afterwards, white people wanted to destroy the Indians, or at least their way of life.

Success or failure?

In the short term the Battle of Little Big Horn was a huge failure for the US army. However, because of the way in which they were defeated, some historians argue that it was actually a long-term success because the defeat led to:
- two forts being built and 2500 army reinforcements sent west
- the pursuit of the Cheyenne and Sioux until most were in their reservations
- the capture of Crazy Horse, who was later killed trying to escape
- Sitting Bull moving his tribes to Canada; however, food shortages forced his return and surrender in 1881
- the Sioux being forced to sell the Black Hills and other land, give up their weapons and horses, and live under military rule.

All of these were reasons for the Indians' eventual defeat.

Now try this

List reasons why the Great Sioux War was such an important event.

Make sure you understand the Great Sioux War and the Battle of Little Big Horn.

Role of the army

Defeating the Plains Indians militarily was just one part of destroying their way of life. You must learn the role of the US army in the suppression of the Indians.

US army

Trained to fight full-scale battles until death if necessary.

Carried rifles and ammunition and had access to other guns.

Based in forts.

Mostly infantry (so were on foot, not horseback).

Had fewer men and fought in territory they did not know.

Soldiers fought as a unit, with set tactics.

Indian warriors

Guerrilla fighters – lived off the land. Skilled at hiding and ambushing.

Used short, sharp raids, not full-scale battles.

All warriors were excellent horsemen.

Relied on traditional weapons, though did have some guns.

Knew the land very well.

Many tribes were enemies and would not unite to fight against the whites.

They recruited spies (or scouts) from tribes that were hostile to other tribes. These scouts passed on valuable military details about Indian positions and tactics.

They built forts along trails and near reservations. This gave them safe places within Indian territory. Indians never managed to capture a fort.

Every soldier had a rifle. The Indians had some guns but relied on traditional weapons – bows and arrows, clubs, spears and knives.

How the US army used military tactics to defeat the Indians

They used total war – against the whole tribe (women, the elderly, children, animals and other belongings). This forced Indians onto reservations.

They attacked Indians during winter when they were most vulnerable. The army had good food and shelter, and could use railroads to move around.

Now try this

Rank the reasons given for the eventual 'victory' of the US army over the Indians. Which do you think was the most important reason and why?

Role of government

You need to know the part played by the US government in destroying the Indians' way of life.

The US government funded soldiers, officers, weapons, uniforms and other equipment.

After the Battle of Little Big Horn, the government tried to either civilise the Indians (by making them behave like white men) or kill them rather than negotiate.

The government gave free land to railroad companies so they could build across the Plains.

The government devised a policy of moving Indians to reservations, which got smaller and smaller.

According to some historians, the government encouraged the destruction of buffalo to make life more difficult for the Indians.

The government encouraged the migration of white Americans onto the Plains because it thought this would make the US more secure. It encouraged the idea of 'Manifest Destiny'.

The government made treaties with the Indians that protected some of their land. However, these treaties were regularly broken by gold miners, ranchers and homesteaders, and the Indians lost trust.

The Dawes Act, 1887

The Dawes General Allotment Act:

- divided Indian reservations into farms for Indian families
- sold any 'left over' land to white settlers.

This was to make Indians behave like white men and farm the land instead of roaming and hunting. Some Indians did become farmers but many refused the land or sold it, which made them dependent on white people for food and shelter.

The Oklahoma land race, 1889

This followed on from the Dawes Act by giving free land to white settlers on a first-come-first-served basis. Thousands charged on horseback and in wagons across Oklahoma to claim pieces of land.

EXAM ALERT!

Remember that the role of the government is not just about the laws that were passed but also about the treatment of the Indians when treaties were broken by settlers and miners and about the deliberate attempts to undermine Indian culture.

Students have struggled with this topic in recent exams – **be prepared!** Result**Plus**

Now try this

List reasons why the government favoured white Americans over Indians.

Reservations

Reservations were first set up to keep Indians and whites apart. Later, they became places that tried to destroy Indian culture by forcing the Indians to behave like white men.

How reservations changed Indian culture

 Tribal chiefs lost their power

The government slowly removed their power so they could no longer govern themselves.

- 1871: chiefs no longer signed treaties.
- Early 1880s: chiefs no longer looked after reservations, councils did.
- 1883: Indians were judged and punished in special courts. These were abolished in 1885 and replaced with US federal law courts.

 Indian children were taught white American values

They were sent to schools where they were punished for using their own language and respecting their culture. They no longer fitted in with their families, but they weren't accepted by the whites, either.

 Indians were not allowed to hunt

This affected their whole social structure and removed men's traditional role. It also affected their clothing and lifestyle.

 Indian beliefs were banned

Putting an end to feasts, dances and ceremonies reduced the power of medicine men, who were an important part of Indian life. Christian missionaries were sent in to 'civilise' them.

 Indians were de-skilled

They were excellent horsemen, hunters and warriors. However, they had no horses on reservations, so they could not hunt buffalo or fight. They refused to learn 'white' skills like ploughing, sowing and reaping.

Life on reservations

Reservation land
Indian reservations were created on land that was least wanted by white Americans. It was not very fertile, didn't contain minerals and would make survival difficult.

Indian agents
The government appointed Indian agents to look after the reservations, but they were often corrupt. Money or rations intended for the Indians often disappeared.

Life on reservations

Living conditions
Rations were poor and crops often failed. Medical care was very poor. Measles and 'flu were common. Many reservation Indians died from them.

Indian Agency Police
Some Indians joined this force to control reservations. In return, they had better food, clothing and shelter than others on the reservation.

Now try this

Jot down all the ways in which Indian reservations changed the traditional Indian way of life.

Indian reservations is an important topic so make sure that you revise it.

Destruction of the buffalo

You need to know all the ways in which buffalo herds were destroyed.

Source of life

In 1840 there were around 13 million buffalo on the Great Plains. By 1885 just 200 survived. Buffalo provided Plains Indians with almost all they needed to survive. Their destruction meant the destruction of this way of life.

Buffalo Bill

William Cody was employed by the Kansas Pacific Railroad Company to clear buffalo from the tracks and supply workers with meat. He claimed he had killed 4280 buffalo in 17 months – hence his nickname.

How buffalo were destroyed

Their habitat was crossed by railroads. Railroad companies used hunters to kill them to feed construction workers.

They were killed by tourists. Special excursion trains brought people onto the Plains to hunt them for sport.

Their hides were made into quality leather goods. White hunters earned good money supplying them.

The grassland they fed on was destroyed or eaten by other animals when settlers built houses, towns, trails and railroads. They also caught diseases spread by the settlers' cattle and horses.

Who was responsible?

Some people suspected that the government encouraged the destruction of buffalo to control the Indians.

- Early on, Indians could leave reservations to hunt, but this was banned in the late 1860s to encourage Indians to live like white people.

- Destroying the buffalo meant Indians were less likely to protest about the loss of their nomadic lifestyle.

- Neither the government nor the army did anything to stop the destruction. In fact, they seem to have encouraged it.

- White Americans enjoyed buffalo hunting and the wealth that hides brought them.

Now try this

Give **five** examples of ways in which the white men destroyed the buffalo.

End of Indian resistance

The way that Indians lived their lives was incompatible with white American society.

What led to the end?

Factors leading to the end of the Indians' way of life include:

- the destruction of buffalo
- railroads
- government reservation policies
- US army actions
- cultural differences with white Americans
- discovery of gold
- cattle trails and ranching
- homesteads on the Plains.

Cultural differences

It's important to remember that Plains Indians were very different from white Americans. They had different:

- attitudes to land and whether it could be owned, bought or sold
- views about farming, nature and the earth
- lifestyles (Indians were nomads)
- beliefs and ways of worship
- methods of warfare
- customs (e.g. whites thought it barbaric that Indians left behind their elderly to die)
- attitudes to leadership (chiefs could not force tribes to obey them).

The role of the railroads

| The railroads played a large part in the destruction of the Indians and their way of life both directly and indirectly. | **Directly**
 • They were built across Indian land.
 • They made it harder for Indians to hunt buffalo and roam freely. | **Indirectly**
 • They took homesteaders to the Plains and cattle to cities – both helped settlement on the Plains to be successful.
 • They created tension – Indians attacked the whites working on them; the whites grew hostile.
 • They brought in the army to protect the railroad workers.
 • They brought in buffalo hunters.
 • They helped the US government fulfil its 'Manifest Destiny'. |

The ghost dance

In 1890, Sioux rations were cut and a drought meant their crops failed. An Indian had a vision that if they all kept dancing, the Great Spirit would bring back the dead and a great flood would carry white people away. More and more Indians began to dance, which worried the Indian agents and whites. The army moved in to stop them. Sitting Bull, who supported the dancing, was killed when Sioux police tried to arrest him. His followers fled south to join the band of Big Foot, who had also fled when the army moved in.

Battle of Wounded Knee

Snow and pneumonia slowed Big Foot's band down and the army caught them. They were taken to Wounded Knee Creek where the army began to disarm them. The Indians started dancing and shooting broke out. After ten minutes, 250 Indians (men, women and children) and 25 soldiers were dead. It was the end of Indian resistance.

Now try this

Jot down the long- and short-term causes of the collapse of Indian resistance.

The Weimar Republic, 1919–22

In November 1918, the Kaiser abdicated. Frederick Ebert and the SPD (Socialists) took control of Germany and declared a republic. In June 1919, the government was told it had to accept the peace terms laid down or the Allies would invade Germany. Meanwhile, leading politicians met (at Weimar, because Berlin was so unsettled) to draw up a new constitution.

Strengths and weaknesses of the Weimar constitution

Strengths

- Most democratic country in the world – everyone could vote (aged over 20) and had equal rights.
- State governments were continued, which allowed state traditions to be maintained.

Both

- Proportional representation meant all parties had a fair share of Reichstag seats. However, this often led to short-lived, weak coalition governments.
- The President could protect Germany in a crisis by making laws without going to the Reichstag, but this could be abused.

Weaknesses

- Free speech gave opposition groups freedom to attack the new government.
- No changes were made to the army or judiciary.
- The voting system made it hard for a government to carry out unpopular policies.
- The President had the power to appoint or dismiss the Chancellor.

The Treaty of Versailles

Loss of territory　　　Payment of £6600 million in reparations

Terms of the Versailles Treaty

Reduce the size of the army and navy　　　Demilitarisation of the Rhineland　　　Admit blame for causing the war – War Guilt Clause

There are two really important things to remember about the Treaty of Versailles.

1 Most Germans hated it! They thought Germany had been 'stabbed in the back' by the Weimar politicians who agreed to the armistice (ceasefire) in November 1918 when most Germans thought Germany was on the brink of winning the war.

2 Payment of reparations and the loss of important industrial areas meant that Germany would have economic problems for years.

Both of these weakened the Weimar Republic and helped its opponents, including the Nazis.

Now try this

Give **five** reasons why the Treaty of Versailles was so unpopular in Germany.

The Treaty of Versailles had a huge impact for years afterwards, so it's really important to revise it carefully.

Opposition groups, 1919–22

The Spartacist League, Freikorps and Nazi Party had differing policies. Make sure you know the differences.

Timeline

German government and opposition groups

11 Nov 1918 First World War fighting ends

June 1919 Leaders sign Treaty of Versailles

Sept 1919 Hitler joins German Workers' Party

Mar 1920 Kapp Putsch in Berlin

9–10 Nov 1918 Kaiser abdicates; Germany now a republic

Jan 1919 Spartacist Revolt in Berlin (communist revolution)

Aug 1919 New constitution for German government set up in Weimar

24 Feb 1920 German Workers' Party changes name to National Socialist German Workers' Party (Nazis)

1921 Hitler takes over from Anton Drexler as leader of the Nazi Party

---

Spartacist Revolt, 1919

The Spartacists took over the government's newspaper and telegraph bureau and tried to organise a general strike in Berlin. The Weimar government sent Freikorps (groups of former soldiers) to put down the revolt. There was street fighting for several days before the revolt ended and Spartacist leaders were shot.

② The Kapp Putsch, 1920

A group of Freikorps, led by Dr Wolfgang Kapp, occupied Berlin. The Weimar government asked the army to suppress the putsch and asked trade unions to organise a general strike. The army refused but trade unions agreed. The general strike caused such chaos that Kapp could not rule Germany and was forced to flee.

Nazi Party, 1920–22

The Nazi Party was a right-wing opposition group with growing membership. It had its own newspapers and held public meetings to spread its ideas. One member, Adolf Hitler, showed great talent for public speaking. The SA (stormtroopers), formed in 1921, were the violent arm of the party, breaking up communist meetings and beating people.

The Spartacists

- The Spartacist League was the name of the German Communist Party.
- Inspired by the 1917 Russian Revolution, it wanted a communist German government
- It was led by Rosa Luxemburg and Karl Liebknecht.

The Freikorps

- Groups of ex-soldiers, mainly right-wing nationalists, used by the Weimar government to squash Spartacist Revolt.
- Disbanded January 1920 when Germany reduced the army, but tried to take power in the Kapp Putsch.

Nazi Party policies, 1920–22

✓ Nationalism
✓ Socialism
✓ Anti-communism
✓ Anti-semitism

Now try this

Write a short explanation of each of the early Nazi policies: nationalism, socialism, anti-communism, anti-semitism.

Hyperinflation, 1923

'Inflation' means the ongoing increase in the price of things, which happens in most economies. 'Hyperinflation' means an extreme increase in prices in a short time.

Gold reserves

The money a country's government prints is supported by its gold reserves. When the government has less gold than money, the value of money goes down and prices go up.

 =   =

The 1923 crisis

> **1914–18**
> The government printed more money to pay for the First World War, but it didn't have more gold.

⬇

> **1918–22**
> The Weimar government printed more money for post-war shortages and asked for longer to pay the first reparations instalment.

⬇

> **January 1923**
> French troops invaded the Ruhr to take reparations payments in goods and raw materials. German workers went on strike.

⬇

> The Weimar government printed more money to pay strikers and make up for loss of coal, steel and iron production.

⬇

> **November 1923**
> The German mark was worthless.

The effects

Prices rose so dramatically that people literally could not carry enough money to buy things. There was widespread panic.

👎 Some people could not afford essentials like bread.

👎 Wages rose, but not as quickly as prices.

👎 Some businesses went bankrupt. (Those that made money took over the struggling ones.)

👎 People with fixed or monthly incomes (e.g. pensioners) suffered most.

👎 Savings became worthless.

👎 People blamed the Weimar government, which made it even more unpopular.

👍 Farmers benefitted, as they were paid more for food.

👍 Some people and businesses could pay off loans and mortgages.

👍 Fixed rents for rooms or shops became very cheap.

Now try this

Make a list of all the ways in which Germany was affected by hyperinflation. Include the groups or types of person most affected.

⬅

The effects of hyperinflation on Germany are important for understanding various topics, so make sure you revise them.

- Remember that middle class people were worst affected.
- Include positive and negative effects of hyperinflation in your list.

Munich Putsch, 1923

The Munich Putsch can be seen as a failure for the Nazi Party in the short term but a success in the long term. You will need to know the reasons why.

Mussolini had successfully taken over the Italian government in 1922.

The Bavarian government was right-wing and didn't like the Weimar government – the Nazis thought the politicians would support them.

Former army leader General Ludendorff was close to Hitler – the Nazis thought he could persuade the German army to support them.

Why did the Nazis try to take power in Munich in November 1923?

The Nazis thought they were ready – Hitler was established as leader, they had 50 000 supporters and the SA.

The Weimar government was unpopular with ordinary Germans especially after it began paying reparations to the French in September.

What happened?

The SA burst into a Munich beer hall where Gustav von Kahr, head of the Bavarian government, was addressing a meeting. Hitler announced they were taking over the government and tried to gain support. The next day Hitler, Ludendorff and about 3000 supporters marched through Munich looking for support. A gun battle with police followed and 16 Nazi supporters were killed. The Putsch had failed; Ludendorff and Hitler were arrested.

The consequences

The Nazi Party was banned and its leaders imprisoned. However, Hitler's trial created public sympathy, and he received the minimum five-year sentence. He served just nine months, using this time to make plans and to write *Mein Kampf*. Failure forced him to rethink tactics – he now knew an armed uprising wouldn't bring him power.

Failure?

- ⊗ The Nazis were not organised.
- ⊗ The police were better prepared.
- ⊗ Too few people in Munich supported the Nazis.
- ⊗ The Bavarian government didn't join the Nazis.
- ⊗ Neither the army nor the police supported the Nazis.
- ⊗ The Putsch appeared a total failure – Hitler was in prison and the Nazi Party was banned.

Success?

- ✓ However, the failure caused Hitler and other Nazi leaders to re-think their tactics.
- ✓ The Nazis gained publicity from the trial, and *Mein Kampf* became a bestseller.
- ✓ People were sympathetic to Nazi ideas. The Party was only banned for a short time and Hitler's sentence was shortened.

Now try this

Give **three** reasons why the Munich Putsch can be seen as a failure and **three** reasons why it can be seen as a success for the Nazi Party.

Weimar recovery, 1924–29

By 1929 the German economy was showing signs of recovering from the disastrous situation of 1923. There were also signs of political stability. However, there were still problems and signs that the recovery would not last.

Gustav Stresemann

Stresemann, who was Chancellor (Aug–Nov 1923) and then Foreign Secretary (1923–29), was responsible for many of the measures shown here.

Gustav Stresemann

Measures taken to boost recovery

Date	Measure	Effect/importance
Nov 1923	Stresemann called off passive resistance and agreed to pay reparations.	• The French withdrew from the Ruhr in 1925. • The policy of fulfilment allowed later negotiations over reparations.
Nov 1923	Stresemann introduced new currency – **Rentenmark**.	• Stabilised currency. • German people showed confidence in it.
1924	Rentenmark converted to **Reichsmark** (backed with gold).	• Gradually restored the value of German money.
1924	Stresemann negotiated **Dawes Plan** with the USA.	• Reorganised reparations. • Brought foreign investment.
1924–30	**US loans**	• Helped pay reparations. • Greatly helped German industry.
1925	**Locarno Treaties**	• Improved relations with UK and France. • Guaranteed borders with Belgium, France and Italy.
1926	Streseman negotiated German entry to **League of Nations**.	• Germany recognised again as great power.
1929	**Young Plan**	• Set timescale and reduced reparations. • France agreed to leave Rhineland early.

Evidence of recovery and remaining problems

👍 There was more stable government through this period...

 👎 but governments were still frequently short-lived coalitions.

👍 There was little support for extremist parties...

👎 but they were still voicing their opinions.

👍 Unemployment fell...

👎 but was still high compared to other countries.

👍 New roads, railways and homes were built...

👎 but this was mainly due to US loans.

👍 By 1928 German industry was back to pre-war levels...

👎 but it slowed down after 1927 and farming was depressed in this period.

👍 By 1930 Germany was one of the leading exporters of manufactured goods...

👎 but it was reliant on US loans.

👍 Germany's importance was again accepted by world powers...

👎 but some treaties (e.g. the Dawes and Young Plans) were unpopular with nationalists.

Now try this

Jot down the policies Stresemann was responsible for.

Stresemann is a key individual. Make sure you have revised his measures and their effects carefully.

The Nazi Party, 1924-28

By 1928, the Nazi Party had more than 100 000 members. This was a massive increase on its early days.

Nazi Party reforms

1 **From local to national**
The Nazi headquarters stayed in Munich but branches were set up all over Germany, with each region or Gau being led by a Gauleiter.

2 **Targeting rural areas**
Especially after 1928, the Nazis focused on winning support from farmers, who were finding times very tough.

3 **Organisations**
Various organisations were set up for different groups: Nazi Students' League, Hitler Youth, Teachers' League and Women's League.

4 **SA**
The image of the SA changed from one of violence and intimidation to one of order and discipline. More young men were encouraged to join.

Rallies: after the first one in Weimar in 1926, they regularly held huge rallies with military-style marches and powerful speeches by Hitler. Rallies were very popular with young supporters.

Meetings: they ran evening classes to train their members in public speaking so they could spread Nazi ideas at meetings and talks.

How the Nazis got their message across 1924–1928

Propaganda: Josef Goebbels skilfully managed Nazi propaganda. He targeted specific groups with specific messages. For example, he found that anti-Jewish propaganda worked best with working class people.

Posters and newspapers: printed propaganda was central to the Nazi message. Posters skilfully got their messages across, while newspapers explained ideas in more depth.

Mein Kampf: Hitler's autobiography, published in 1925, promoted his aims: removing Jews from Germany, destroying communism and expanding Germany. It became a bestseller.

Nazi support in the 1920s

👍 Young people.

👍 Skilled workers.

👍 Farmers.

👍 Middle and upper classes who feared communism.

EXAM ALERT!

Be clear about the ways the Nazis used legal tactics to gain support in this period.

Students have struggled with this topic in recent exams – **be prepared!** ResultsPlus

---

Now try this

Jot down four reasons why propaganda was so successful at winning support for the Nazis.

Make sure you know the different types of propaganda used and who it appealed to.

The Great Depression

By 1932 six million Germans were unemployed (compared to 0.8 million in 1928).

Economic impact on Germany

Wall Street Crash

Wall Street Crash, USA, October 1929
US companies lost billions of dollars in value overnight. Many banks and businesses were ruined.

⬇

The Great Depression
The Crash triggered a worldwide recession. Germany suffered very badly.

⬇

US stopped lending money to Germany and demanded all loans be repaid.

The Depression in Berlin

German businesses
- Had to pay back loans.
- Had no more investment from the US.
- Had to pay increased taxes to government.
- Worldwide, no one had money to buy goods, so markets dried up.

German government
- Couldn't borrow money from the US.
- Refused to print more money.
- Increased taxes.
- Made cuts in unemployment benefit.
- Government workers had wages cut and some lost their jobs.

German people
- Businesses reduced staff or closed.
- Millions of workers and farm labourers lost their jobs.
- Young people were badly affected by job losses.
- With no work, and benefits slashed, families suffered terrible poverty.

Political impact

The Depression had a deep political impact.

- The Weimar government was blamed for German dependence on US loans.
- It highlighted a lack of strong leadership (Stresemann had died just before the Crash).
- The two main parties in the coalition government (Centre Party and SDP) could not agree how to solve the crisis.

- President Hindenburg used Article 48 of the constitution to pass laws without Reichstag agreement. In effect, Germany was no longer a democracy.
- New economic policies were very unpopular.
- Extremist parties (especially the Communists and Nazis) became more popular.

Now try this

Jot down at least **three** ways in which the Depression was different from hyperinflation.

 Be sure you understand the difference between hyperinflation in 1923 and the Depression in the 1930s.

The Nazi Party, 1929–32

The Nazis went from winning 12 seats in the 1928 Reichstag elections to 107 seats in 1930 and 230 seats in July 1932. You need to know how the Nazis won this support and who voted for them.

Propaganda methods

By now, Goebbels was a master of propaganda and skilfully used many different methods to spread the Nazi message.

 Posters   Radio   Rallies

 Newspapers   Parades and marches

Hitler's image

Hitler was the focus of much propaganda and appeared on posters and in newspapers. His speeches were central to rallies and parades. He was portrayed as a 'superman' who could end the German crisis. He blamed Weimar politicians, communists and Jews for all of Germany's problems.

The SA's image

By 1932 the image of the SA (brownshirts) had improved and they had about 600 000 members. They attracted young, unemployed people who admired their ordered and disciplined parades through towns and cities. At the same time, they continued to disrupt the meetings of rival groups (especially the Communist Party).

Who voted for the Nazis in July 1932?

Many people voted for them because they shared their dislikes (of communism, for example) and believed Nazi propaganda about groups like Jews and gypsies.

Women

Agricultural workers

Middle classes

Working classes

Upper classes and big business

Young people

Now try this

Jot down reasons why people voted for Hitler in 1932.

Hitler becomes Chancellor

The actions of three key people resulted in Hitler becoming Chancellor. You will need to know who these people were and the sequence of political events.

Timeline

Political events, 1932

May 1932 Hindenburg replaces Chancellor Heinrich Brüning with von Papen

Nov 1932 Von Papen calls another election and Centre Party loses more seats. The Nazis also lose some seats but are still the largest party

28 Jan 1933 Lack of support forces von Schleicher's resignation

Mar / Apr 1932 Hindenburg beats Hitler in Presidential election but Hitler gains support

Jul 1932 Von Papen's Centre Party holds Reichstag elections to gain support but loses seats. Nazis become largest party, but Hitler not made Chancellor

Dec 1932 Hindenburg removes von Papen and makes von Schleicher Chancellor

30 Jan 1933 Hitler becomes Chancellor

Paul von Hindenburg

Hindenburg, a hero of the First World War, became president in April 1925. In the Depression crisis, he used his emergency powers to rule without the Reichstag after 1930. He appointed his friend Franz von Papen, then his adviser Kurt von Schleicher, Chancellor in 1932. However, neither could form a government. Even though Hindenburg was politically right wing, he distrusted Hitler and thought the Nazis were too violent. When the Nazis became the biggest party he refused to appoint Hitler Chancellor, by the end of January 1933, von Papen persuaded him that Hitler was his only option. He therefore made Hitler Chancellor on condition that von Papen was Vice-Chancellor and there were only a few Nazis in the Cabinet. He thought this would keep Hitler under control.

Franz von Papen

Von Papen (Chancellor from May to November 1932) led the Centre Party.
- He was furious when von Schleicher became Chancellor and started negotiating with Hitler.
- He persuaded his friend Hindenburg to appoint Hitler after von Schleicher resigned, believing Hitler could be controlled.
- He became Vice-Chancellor to Hitler 1933–34.

Kurt von Schleicher

Von Schleicher was the army's chief political adviser to President Hindenburg.
- He advised Hindenburg not to re-appoint von Papen in November (he thought it would cause communist and Nazi violence on the streets). The President made von Schleicher Chancellor instead.
- He couldn't form a government and lost the support of Hindenburg. He resigned believing von Papen would succeed him.

Hitler becomes Chancellor

After the political manoeuvring of Hindenberg, von Papen and von Schleicher, Hitler became Chancellor on 30 January 1933. Hindenberg and von Papen were convinced that they would be able to use Hitler initially, and then get rid of him later.

Now try this

Jot down reasons why Hitler was able to become Chancellor of Germany.

 Remember to include direct and indirect reasons.

Key events, 1933

A fire, an act, an election and a decree all had serious consequences in 1933.

The Reichstag Fire

On 27 February 1933, the Reichstag building was burned down. Found inside was Dutch communist Marius van der Lubbe, who confessed. Hitler accused the German Communist Party of trying to take over the government and arrested 4000 communists. On 8 February Hindenburg (persuaded by Hitler) passed an emergency decree. Some people believe the fire was started by the Nazis.

Emergency decree

Thanks to the Decree for the Protection of the People and the State, the state could now:

- arrest and detain people without trial for as long as they wanted
- search and confiscate property
- read post and listen to telephone calls
- censor the press
- stop people organising meetings.

The election, March 1933

The Nazis won more seats than ever but still had under half the total rather than the two-thirds majority needed to change the constitution.

The Enabling Act, March 1933

This gave Hitler the power to make any law he wanted for four years without the consent of the Reichstag. The Act meant that Germany was no longer a democracy.

Passing the Act

The Enabling Act was passed by 444 votes to 91. But how did this happen?

- An emergency decree meant the 81 communist members couldn't take up their seats.
- Hitler made deals with the National and Centre parties.
- The SA surrounded the meeting and threatened opposition politicians.

What happened next?

The Enabling Act allowed Hitler to get rid of opposition to the Nazis.

State parliaments: these were closed down on 31 March 1933 and reorganised with Nazi majorities. They were completely abolished in January 1934.

Trade unions: these were replaced with the German Labour Front. Many union officials were arrested on 2 May 1933.

Other political parties: in May 1933 the SDP and Communist Party offices and funds were taken by the Nazis. In July 1933, other political parties were banned.

Now try this

Jot down at least **three** reasons why the Enabling Act was important in leading to Hitler having total control of Germany.

Make sure you know how the Act was passed and the powers it gave to Hitler.

Key events, 1934

The Night of the Long Knives, the death of Hindenburg and the cult of the Führer all helped the Nazis to consolidate power.

Night of the Long Knives

On 30 June 1934, Hitler arranged a meeting with Ernst Röhm and other SA leaders. These leaders were arrested by the SS, taken to Munich and shot. In the following days others, such as Gregor Strasser and Kurt von Schleicher, were killed. As a result:

- few people were left to rival Hitler
- the army swore allegiance to Hitler personally in August
- the SS was established as a major force.

Why did this happen?

- The SA was no longer needed for the Nazis to maintain power.
- The army wanted the SA to be controlled, and was powerful enough to overthrow Hitler if he didn't do something.
- The SA had nearly 2 million violent members and was a threat to Hitler.
- The SA leaders had bad reputations.
- There was an ongoing power struggle between Heinrich Himmler (the SS leader) and Röhm (the SA leader).

EXAM ALERT!

Be clear about the role of the SA in the Nazis' rise to power and the importance of the Night of the Long Knives.

Students have struggled with this topic in recent exams – **be prepared!**   ResultsPlus

Death of Hindenburg

President Hindenburg was the only person senior to Hitler. In August 1934, he died. Within hours, Hitler declared himself Führer (leader), and took on the president's powers.

Cult of the Führer

Portrayed as a God-like leader.

Sacrificed his own happiness to serve Germany.

A soldier of the people who could make Germany great again.

People could see and meet him on his frequent tours.

Ein Volk, ein Reich, ein Führer!

He featured in much Nazi propaganda, and gave speeches at rallies and on the radio.

People swore allegiance to him personally and gave the 'Heil Hitler' salute.

He gave his trusted supporters wide-ranging powers.

The slogan reads: One people, one nation, one leader!

Now try this

List all the reasons why Hitler was able to expand his power between January 1933 and August 1934.

Nazi use of terror

The Nazis used a combination of laws, terror and brainwashing to control the German people. It is important to revise them all so you can give a full answer about ALL methods of Nazi control.

Nazi police state

The Nazi police state used many different methods of control.

- New laws made it a crime to listen to a foreign radio station, say anything against Hitler or tell an anti-Nazi joke.
- The SS (the main enforcers of the police state) arrested anyone who broke the new laws or opposed the Nazis. This was called 'protective custody'.
- The Gestapo (the secret police) spied on people by reading their mail and listening to phone calls.
- Block wardens were each given 40 households to spy on for suspicious behaviour.
- People were encouraged to inform on friends, family, work colleagues and neighbours.
- Law courts were under total Nazi control, with judges swearing loyalty to Hitler. There was no trial by jury.
- Many prisoners were taken to concentration camps.

The SS

- SS = *Schulz-Staffel* (protection squad).
- Was created in 1925 as a small group of 'bodyguards' for Hitler.
- After 1929, was led by Himmler.
- Grew under Himmler; acted as the police of the Nazi state.
- Had unlimited powers to search property, and arrest and imprison people without trial.
- Was supported by the Gestapo and block wardens who spied on people.
- Ran the concentration and death camps.
- Helped get rid of the SA in the Night of the Long Knives.

What's the difference?

- The SA (the brownshirts) were dominant **before** the Nazis came to power. The SS (the blackshirts) were dominant **after** 1933.
- Concentration camps, used from 1933, were mainly for political prisoners. Death camps, after 1941, were extermination centres, mainly for Jews.

Concentration camps

Most prisoners were taken to these for 'questioning', imprisonment, torture and re-education. The first one was established in 1933 at Dachau, but they soon developed all over Germany. Conditions were bad. Inmates were brutally treated and forced to do hard labour. Many died from disease or starvation.

Now try this

Jot down **three** ways in which the SS were used to control the German people.

Any answer about how the Nazis controlled Germany should feature the SS.

Censorship and propaganda

To make sure that people had access to only their ideas and beliefs, the Nazis used propaganda to spread their ideas, and censorship to silence opposition.

Josef Goebbels

Goebbels played a central role as Nazi Minister of Enlightenment and Propaganda. He was very skilful at spreading Nazi ideas. He controlled newspapers, the radio, book publishing, films and the arts.

Methods of censorship

- Public burning of books by Jewish writers or others who disagreed with Nazi views.
- Radio producers, playwrights, filmmakers and newspapers were told what to say.
- Newspapers opposing the Nazis were closed.
- Only radios that couldn't receive foreign stations were made.

Methods of propaganda

Hitler featured in lots of propaganda, either with a photograph or his name or title.

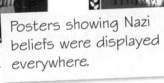

Posters showing Nazi beliefs were displayed everywhere.

The cinema showed propaganda films, but mainly entertainment films that had subtle Nazi messages.

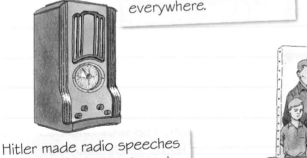

Hitler made radio speeches which were played through loudspeakers in factories, cafés and on the streets. Entertainment programmes contained Nazi ideas and beliefs.

The Nazis encouraged artists and playwrights to produce work highlighting Nazi ideas. Modern art and culture such as jazz music were banned.

Huge rallies and military parades were held, projecting a power and strength that would either make Germans proud of their country or fill them with terror depending on their viewpoint.

Now try this

Jot down a list of all the ways you can think of in which the Nazis spread their ideas.

Propaganda was a central feature of Nazi Germany, so make sure you revise how it was used in different situations and contexts.

The Churches

The Nazis were against religion. They wanted total loyalty to Hitler and his beliefs. You need to know how Hitler tried to control the Churches and how some Church leaders opposed him.

Nazi vs Christian beliefs

Nazi beliefs	Christian beliefs
Hitler as all-powerful leader.	God as ultimate authority.
Ayran racial superiority.	Everyone equal in the eyes of God.
War, military discipline and violence important.	Peace is what everyone should strive for.
Dominance of the strong over the weak.	The strong should look after the weak.

The Catholic Church

Hitler worried that the Catholic Church would oppose him because Catholics:

- were loyal to the Pope
- usually supported the Centre Party
- sent their children to Catholic schools and the Catholic youth organisation.

By 1934, despite an initial agreement (see below), Catholic schools had to remove Christian symbols from classrooms and were later closed. In 1937, the Catholic youth organisations became illegal. Priests opposing the Nazis were sent to concentration camps. However, Catholic churches were still full and arrested priests were treated as martyrs.

The Protestant churches

Reich Church

- Founded in 1933
- Made up of about 2000 Protestant churches
- Supported the Nazis
- Led by Ludwig Müller
- Some members wore Nazi uniform

Confessional Church

- Founded in 1934
- Made up of about 6000 Protestant churches
- Opposed the Nazis
- Led by Martin Niemöller
- Were repressed by the Nazis

Catholic Concordat, July 1933

Hitler let Catholics worship and run their own schools and organisations. In return, the Pope stayed out of German politics. The agreement broke down within a year.

'With Burning Anxiety', 1937

Many people criticised Pope Pius XI for not speaking out against Hitler. However, in 1937 he issued a statement known as 'With Burning Anxiety' criticising Nazi policies.

Now try this

Jot down **three** ways in which the Nazis were able to control the Churches in Germany.

Opposition 1

Although no one really knows how many German people opposed the Nazis, there were some incredibly brave people who acted against them. Here we will look at opposition from the Church, young people and the army.

Opposition to the Nazis

There were many ways people resisted Nazi rule, such as listening to banned music or telling anti-Nazi jokes, hiding Jews, speaking out against the regime or trying to kill Hitler. You can include all types of opposition in your answers to general questions on 'opposition'. In general, though, there was very little open opposition to the regime and it's important you revise the reasons for this.

Lack of opposition

There were several reasons why there was a lack of opposition to the Nazis.

- Many people resisted privately, not openly.
- Nazi policies improved many Germans' lives.
- Opposition groups were banned.
- People feared the SS, the Gestapo and concentration camps.
- There was a large number of informers.
- There was also genuine support for Hitler.

Church opposition

Although Hitler tried to suppress opposition from the Churches, there were still Catholic priests and Protestant ministers and pastors who preached against Nazi policies. Thousands were arrested and sent to concentration camps where many died.

- In 1941, the Action T4 euthanasia programme ended when the Catholic Cardinal Galen spoke out against it.
- Pastor Dietrich Bonhoeffer spoke out, particularly against Nazi Jewish policies. He was arrested, sent to a concentration camp and executed.
- Many Protestant churches joined the Confessional Church in opposition to the Nazi-supporting Reich Church.

Pastor Martin Niemöller

Niemöller originally supported Hitler.
- He changed his views when the Reich Church was set up.
- In 1934, he set up the Confessional Church.
- He frequently spoke out against the Nazis.
- In July 1937 he was arrested and sent to prison for seven months. He continued attacking Nazi policies when he was released.
- He was arrested again and spent seven years in concentration camps until the end of the Second World War.

Now try this

Give **three** examples of how some Christians opposed the Nazi regime.

Opposition 2

Some Germans opposed to the Nazis set up secret groups, and after the outbreak of the Second World War, there was also opposition from within the German army.

The White Rose Group

This group was set up at Munich University by Hans and Sophie Scholl and Kurt Huber.

- The white rose was a symbol of justice; the group was non-violent.
- Hans had seen the murder of Jews and other non-Aryans on the Eastern Front.
- The group let people know about the atrocities that were happening.
- It created and distributed leaflets opposing the Nazis and the war.
- All three leaders (plus other members) were eventually caught and executed.

The Edelweiss Pirates

These were small groups who opposed the Hitler Youth. They eventually set up a national organisation.

- Boys wore check shirts and dark trousers and girls wore make-up and permed their hair.
- The edelweiss was their symbol.
- They read and listened to banned media, including jazz, and wrote anti-Nazi graffiti.
- They spread Allied propaganda leaflets.
- They gave shelter to army deserters.
- They frequently attacked members of the Hitler Youth and in 1944 they killed the head of the Cologne Gestapo.

- Some were caught and hanged.

Army opposition

Army members swore an oath of loyalty to Hitler. During the 1930s they showed few signs of opposition. This changed in the 1940s because:

- the army suffered defeats on the Eastern Front
- many soldiers saw, and didn't like, SS brutality.

Opposition from the army was Hitler's greatest fear because of their access to weapons and millions of highly trained men.

> Operation Valkyrie was also known as the July Plot.

Operation Valkyrie

Appalled by his experiences on the Eastern Front, Count von Stauffenberg devised 'Operation Valkyrie'. This was a plot to assassinate Hitler, using a bomb in a briefcase.

At a military conference in East Prussia on 20 July 1944, von Stauffenberg tried to blow up Hitler. The bomb exploded, but Hitler was protected by a table. Von Stauffenberg, along with 5746 others (including 19 generals and 27 colonels), was executed for his role. This highlights the deep opposition to Hitler from within the army towards the end of the war.

Now try this

Jot down **three** types of opposition to the Nazis and **one** example of a person or group who opposed the Nazis in this way.

> Always give good examples to back up your answers!

Policies towards women

Women in the Weimar Republic had equal voting rights and educational opportunities. Many became professionals (doctors and lawyers) and some enjoyed modern fashion. The Nazis had a very different view of the role of women and some German women agreed with them.

The Nazis' ideal woman

Natural appearance – long hair tied back, no make-up.

Wore traditional clothes.

Fair haired and blue eyed (Aryan).

Sturdily built (for child bearing).

Non-drinker/smoker.

Would marry and have many children.

Believed in the Nazi ideas of *kinder, küche, kirche* (children, kitchen, church).

Would not go to university.

Would stay at home rather than go to work.

Front cover from *Women's Viewpoint*, the official Nazi magazine for women. Published on Mother's Day in 1939.

Nazi policies on women

Policy	Was it a success?
Women should not work, especially those who were married. Many professional women lost their jobs and men were favoured for employment.	During 1933–36 the number of employed married women fell. It rose again because of the workforce shortage during the war. Many employers preferred women because their wages were two-thirds those of men.
Women should get married. The Law for the Encouragement of Marriage, 1933, lent money to couples if the wife left work.	The number of marriages did increase, but it's not clear if this was due to Nazi policy.
Women should have at least four children. (Couples were let off one-quarter of their marriage loan repayments for each child they had). The German Women's Enterprise gave women medals for having children (bronze for four to five, silver for six to seven, gold for eight or more), and ran classes and radio programmes on household topics.	The German Women's Enterprise had six million members, which implies that many women welcomed Nazi policies. The birth rate did increase but this may have been because the economy was improving rather than Nazi policies. Few women had more than two children.

Now try this

What can you learn about Nazi views of women from the picture above?

The first question on the exam will always be an inference question asking what you can work out from a source.

Nazi education

The Nazis wanted to make German children loyal Nazis and prepare them for their future roles in the Third Reich. You need to learn the two main aspects of this: education and youth movements.

Aims of Nazi education policies

To prepare girls to be good wives and mothers.

To turn boys into strong soldiers who would fight for Germany.

To create loyal Nazis.

To teach Nazi beliefs about race.

To put across key Nazi ideals.

To glorify Germany and the Nazi Party.

Nazi control of education

Schools	Teachers	Subjects	Propaganda
• Children had to attend state school until aged 14. • Separate schools for girls and boys. • Optional schools after age 14: National Political Educational Institutes and Adolf Hitler Schools. • All schools followed a set curriculum – different for girls and boys.	• Compulsory for teachers to be Nazi Party members. • Those who didn't teach Nazi ideas were sacked. • Teachers' camps taught them how to use Nazi ideas in their teaching. • Nearly all teachers joined the Nazi Teachers' Association.	• 15% of time on PE to ensure healthy and strong population. • Girls were taught domestic skills, while boys were taught science and military skills. • Both sexes were taught the traditional subjects: German, History, Geography and Maths. • New subjects: Race studies and Eugenics were taught to both sexes.	• All lessons began and ended with the Hitler salute. • From 1935 all textbooks had to be approved by the Nazi Party. • Traditional subjects were rewritten to glorify Germany, including great German writers and History. • Racial ideas and anti-semitism were embedded within subjects.

Now try this

Jot down **three** reasons why control of education was so important to the Nazis.

Nazi youth groups

There were four Nazi youth groups: Young German Folk (boys aged 10–14), Young Girls (girls aged 10–14), Hitler Youth (boys aged 14–18), and League of German Maidens (girls aged 14–18). Meetings and activities took place after school, at weekends and in the holidays.

How youth groups were used

- They ensured that the Nazis had control over children when they weren't at school.
- All other youth groups (political and religious) were closed down.
- Like schools, they concentrated on creating loyal Nazis and preparing children for their future roles.
- From 1936 the Hitler Youth Law made it difficult not to join one. From 1939 joining was compulsory.
- From 1940, the groups became involved in helping the war effort.
- By 1943, the Hitler Youth had become a military reserve – members as young as 12 joined the army.

Problems

- Not all youngsters joined (for example, members of the Edelweiss Pirates).
- Some children found the activities boring, especially as they focused more and more on the military.
- Groups altered family life because they took up time at weekends and evenings.
- Some parents didn't like them because they taught children that their first allegiance was to Hitler and they encouraged children to spy.
- Conscription (having to join the army) meant there was a shortage of adult leaders.

Examples of youth group activities

Boys
Shooting
Military drills
Signalling
Military-style camps
Helping the fire brigade during the war
Formed military brigades to defend Berlin in 1945

Both
Hiking and camping
Learning about Hitler
Learning about racial superiority
Singing patriotic songs
Sport and competitions
Taking part in Nazi marches and rallies
Reporting people who made anti-Nazi comments
Collecting for Winterhilfe (a charity)

Girls
Cookery
Housework
Needlework and craft
Learning what to look for in a good husband
Learning about babies and childcare

Now try this

Jot down **three** similarities and **three** differences between youth groups for girls and boys.

Questions could focus on similarities **and/or** differences.

Economic changes

In 1933 Germany was suffering badly from the Depression, so economic changes were vital. You need to learn the Nazi economic policies and how they reduced unemployment.

New Plan, 1933–37

New Plan, 1933–37

The New Plan was run by Dr Hjalmar Schacht, Minister of the Economy.

- It aimed to reduce unemployment and make Germany self-sufficient.
- It successfully limited imports.
- The plan made trade agreements with other countries for vital supplies in return for German goods.
- The plan successfully increased trade and production (and therefore provided more jobs). Schacht lost his job in 1937 because of a disagreement about rearmament.

Four Year Plan, 1936 onwards

Four Year Plan, 1936 onwards

This plan was run by Hermann Göring.

- The whole economy was geared towards rearmament and preparing for war.
- The plan cost millions but wasn't a success at making Germany less dependent on foreign imports for raw materials.
- It used prisoners in labour and concentration camps as a labour force.
- It created more jobs in manufacturing weapons, tanks, ships and aircraft.
- It increased the army from 100 000 men in 1933 to 1 400 000 in 1939.

National Labour Service (RAD)

This was started by the Weimar government and continued by the Nazis.

- From July 1935, it was compulsory for all men aged 18–25 to serve six months on this scheme.
- They worked on the Job Creation Schemes and other public works such as draining marshes.
- Many hated RAD: the pay was low, the hours long and the work boring.

Built 7000 km of autobahns.

Subsidised private firms like car manufacturers.

Job Creation Schemes

Constructed public buildings.

Construction for the 1936 Olympics.

Invisible unemployment

Official government figures showed unemployment was falling but they did not include:

- Jews being forced out of jobs

- women being dismissed or leaving their jobs

- unmarried men under 25 doing National Labour Service

- opponents of the regime sent to concentration camps.

Now try this

Jot down at least **three** ways in which the Nazis reduced unemployment.

Make sure you understand the ways in which the Nazis reduced unemployment. This often features in exam questions.

German people's lives

Some people's lives improved and some people's didn't. When you answer questions on this topic, it is important that you do not generalise.

Schemes to improve workers' lives

> **German Labour Front**
> The *Deutsche Arbeitsfront* (DAF) replaced trade unions.
> Workers had to be members. It ran several schemes.

Strength through Joy (KdF)	Beauty of Labour (SdA)	The Volkswagen (people's car)
This aimed to increase productivity by making workers happy. It provided low-cost or free activities (e.g. concerts, holidays) for hard workers.	This aimed to improve conditions by reducing noise in workplaces, providing canteens and even building swimming pools. However, workers had to help construct these in their spare time, so it wasn't very popular.	Workers paid five marks a week towards buying a car. No cars had been bought by 1939, so the money went towards rearmament. It was not refunded to workers.

Were workers better off?

Better off ✓	Worse off ✗
More jobs created, most men in work.	Few rights – trade unions abolished.
Average weekly wages rose from 86 marks (1932) to 109 marks (1939).	Cost of living rose, which cancelled out wage increase.
Beauty of Labour – better conditions such as canteens and sports facilities.	Average working hours increased from 43 hours per week (1933) to 47 (1939).
Strength through Joy – better leisure activities for workers.	Few workers could afford the best activities and holidays provided by Strength through Joy.

Were other people better off?

Most people struggled with food shortages at different times. In addition:

 Women: some wanted to work. Others were happy to stay at home and have children.

 Farmers: they benefitted from rising food prices. Some had help from the Labour Service. Others lost workers to the army and factories.

 Businesses: some benefitted from the closure of Jewish businesses. Large businesses had extra opportunities due to rearmament and subsidies. Some used forced labour from concentration camps. There were no trade union problems but some did resent Nazi controls.

Now try this

Jot down **three** reasons that support and **three** reasons that don't support the statement 'Germans benefitted from rising living standards 1933–39'.

 When questions ask for an opinion make sure you give one. There is no right or wrong answer but you must give reasons for your views.

Ideas and policies on race

Hitler was keen to increase the number of 'pure' Germans (Aryans) who were blond-haired, blue-eyed, tall and athletic, and who would work hard, join the army or have children.

Nazi racial hierarchy

Aryans
The 'master race'.

Other white Western Europeans
Seen as fellow humans but lower than Aryans.

Eastern Europeans
Slavs – seen as 'sub-human'.

Black people and gypsies
Both seen as 'sub-human' and 'work-shy' (lazy).

Jews
Seen as lowest of 'sub-human' races and blamed for Germany's problems.

How the race grew

'Race farms' were set up where Aryan men and women met to have Aryan children. The SS were central to the Nazi master race, as they only recruited Aryans and were only allowed to marry Aryan women.

An idealised Aryan family

Treatment of untermenschen

At this time, a few black people, about 30 000 gypsies and half a million Jews lived in Germany.

- In 1935, the Nuremburg Laws banned Aryans from marrying gypsies, black people or Jews.
- Mixed race children were sterilised.
- In 1938, all gypsies had to be registered.
- Many gypsies were sent to concentration camps. The number who died isn't known.

Untermenschen meant 'inferior' or 'sub-human'. Nazis classed all Slavs, gypsies, black people and Jews as untermenschen. They were definitely not part of Hitler's pure race.

'Non-perfect' Aryans

Not all Aryans were acceptable to the Nazis.

- Mentally ill people were put into 'care homes' and sterilised.
- The same happened to mentally or physically disabled people, but they were later killed.
- Homosexuals (mainly men) were put in concentration camps. They were subjected to medical experiments to 'correct' their sexuality.
- Vagrants were seen as 'work-shy'. Many were put in concentration camps.

Now try this

Write a short summary of the Nazis' beliefs about a 'master race'.

Treatment of Jews, 1933-39

The Nazis saw the Jews as a threat, so they made life very difficult for them. You will need to know how the Nazis persecuted the Jews during this period.

Timeline

1933-39 policies

1933
SA organised one-day boycott of Jewish shops, lawyers and doctors. Some property damage.
Jews working in government jobs (including some teachers) were sacked.
Jewish actors and musicians were banned from public performance.

1934
Jews were banned from public places like parks and swimming pools.

1935
The Nuremburg Laws denied Jews German citizenship (which meant they lost the right to vote).
Jews were banned from marrying Aryans.
Jews were forbidden to join the army.

1936
Jews were banned or restricted from professions – vets, accountants, teachers, dentists, nurses.

1937
More Jewish businesses were 'Aryanised' – taken over by Aryans.

1938
From April, Jews had to register their property.
Jewish doctors, dentists and lawyers were forbidden to treat or work for Aryans.
Passports of Jews had to be stamped with a 'J'.
Jews had to add 'Israel' or 'Sarah' to their names.
Kristallnacht (November): Jewish shops and synagogues set on fire or vandalised; 20 000 Jews arrested, 91 killed. Jewish community had to pay a fine and pay for the damage to their property.
Jews were barred from owning or managing businesses.

Why Jews?

Jews were the subject of Nazi anti-semitic propaganda from the earliest years of the party. However, the Nazis didn't invent anti-semitism. There was already a long history of Jews being persecuted throughout Europe and in Germany.

EXAM ALERT!

Remember that many people might not have agreed with this persecution but let it happen because they were afraid of getting into trouble or because they liked other aspects of Nazi policies.

Students have struggled with this topic in recent exams – **be prepared!** ResultsPlus

Reasons why Jews were persecuted

- Associated with communism (Karl Marx was Jewish).
- Jealous of success – many Jews were professionals or owned businesses.
- Used as scapegoats for Germany's problems.
- Suspicious of a different religion.
- Blamed for Germany's defeat in First World War and the Treaty of Versailles (especially as some politicians involved were Jewish).

Kristallnacht

Now try this

Give examples of how persecution of Jews increased between 1933 and 1939.

Treatment of Jews, 1939–45

During the Second World War, Jews were forced out of Germany and millions were killed in the countries that were conquered.

Timeline

The Final Solution

1939
First ghettos opened in Poland. These were walled parts of a city where all Jews were forced to live. They were overcrowded, with little food allowed in. Thousands died from disease or starvation.

June 1941
Germany invaded Russia. *Einsatzgruppen* units followed the German army, rounding up Jews, marching them to places where they were forced to dig a huge grave, then shot.

Summer 1941
Nazi leaders decide on a 'final solution' – to murder all Jews in German-occupied countries.

September 1941
All Jews in the German Reich were ordered to wear the yellow Star of David.

January 1942
Leading Nazis met at the Wannsee Conference to work out the details of the 'final solution'.

1942–45
Millions of Jews from all over German-occupied Europe were transported to death camps in Poland. Many (especially those unable to work such as the elderly, children and pregnant women) were killed straight away in gas chambers and their bodies burned in ovens or left in mass pits. Others worked in harsh conditions with little food. Some were used for medical experiments. By the end of the war, some six million Jews had been worked to death, gassed or shot.

The Second World War

In January 1939 the Reich Central Office for Jewish Emigration was set up to force Jews to leave Germany. However, the outbreak of war changed the 'Jewish problem'.

- Germany took over places where they had planned to forcibly move German Jews.
- These new parts of the Reich included millions more Jews.
- World opinion mattered less, so treatment could be more extreme.

How could the Holocaust happen?

- People feared the Gestapo and SS, who severely punished anyone helping Jews or speaking out against the Nazi regime.
- Some didn't know what was happening (the death camps were mainly in Poland, not Germany).
- Since the 1920s, and even more so after Hitler became Chancellor, the Nazis had bombarded people with anti-semitic propaganda in cinemas, posters, newspapers, school books and on the radio. Some Germans believed this and supported Nazi policies.

A Nazi concentration camp

Now try this

Give examples of the ways in which the Nazis' treatment of the Jews changed after 1939.

It's always good to give examples to back up your answers.

Source skills 1

Unit 3 of GCSE History is very different from Units 1 and 2. It's about how sources are used by historians. This section will help you to revise the skills you need.

Your exam

- Your paper has a collection of sources – between six and eight.
- These sources could be images or text.
- They all relate to your topic, but in different ways.
- You answer all five questions.
- Each question tests a particular skill.
- The questions are always in the same order.

What skills will I need?

There are five skills, one for each question.

 Making inferences from sources.

 Analysing sources for message or purpose.

 Cross-referencing sources.

 Evaluating the usefulness or reliability of sources.

 Evaluating a hypothesis.

Question 1: inference

An inference is something that can be worked out from a source but isn't directly shown in the source. Inference questions will ask things like:

> What can you learn from Source A about …

You can demonstrate inference skills by:

- ✓ thinking about what is suggested or implied by the source
- ✓ explaining how the source helped you to make that inference
- ✗ not just describing what the source shows.

Question 1 is worth 6 marks

- Make two inferences.
- Support each inference.

Supporting your inference means backing up the point you make. You can do this by showing how something in the source led you to make that inference.

Question 2: analysis

Analysis means you should explain the message the source is trying to give. Analysis questions will ask things like:

> What impression has the artist tried to give of …
> Explain your answer, using Source B.

> How has the author conveyed his message? Explain your answer, using Source B.

You can demonstrate analysis skills by:

- ✓ thinking about why the source was created and how the creator gets their message across
- ✓ thinking about what has been included or left out and why.

Question 2 is worth 8 marks

- Identify the message of the source.
- Explain how that message is given.

For visual sources think about colours, positions of things, and use of light. For written sources, think about the language chosen, details given and the order things are presented in.

Now try this

Jot down what you need to do for:
(a) inference questions. (b) analysis questions.

Source skills 2

Unit 3 isn't about remembering facts, it's about interpreting information. You use what you know about a topic to help you interpret.

What to learn

The topic knowledge you need to revise is on pages 95–98 if you studied *The transformation of surgery c1845–c1918* or on pages 99–102 if you studied *Protest, law and order in the twentieth century*. However, revising the source skills for these is more important, as that is what the exam is testing.

Time management

In your exam you will need to answer all five questions in 1 hour 15 minutes. Question 5 gives the most marks, so leave 25 minutes to answer it. That means you have 5 minutes for Question 1, 10 minutes for Question 2 and 15 minutes each for Questions 3 and 4. This gives you 5 minutes spare to check your answers at the end.

Question 3: cross-referencing

Cross-referencing is about comparing a number of sources. Common question types include:

> 'Study Sources A, B and C. How far do these sources agree about …'

> 'Study Sources C, D and E. How far do these sources support the view that …'

You can demonstrate cross-referencing skills by:

- ✓ listing the ways in which the sources agree with each other or support the statement
- ✓ listing the ways the sources disagree or don't support the statement
- ✓ making an overall judgement about how far they agree.

Question 4: usefulness or reliability

Utility means usefulness. These questions ask about how useful / reliable sources are for the historian.

> 'Which of Sources D or E is more valuable to the historian …'

> 'How useful are Sources C and D as evidence for a historian studying …'

You can demonstrate usefulness and reliability skills by:

- ✓ thinking about what information in the source is relevant to the topic of the question
- ✓ considering reliability – who created the source and why? Do you trust the source?

Question 3 is worth 10 marks

- Explain how far the sources agree *and* disagree.
- Explain your judgement in terms of both **content** and **reliability**.

Taking both content and reliability into account will further improve your answer.

Question 4 is worth 10 marks

- Judge the usefulness of the content of each source, taking account of how that is affected by the source's reliability.
- Judge which source is more useful.

The best answers do both these things.

Remember: a source may be very useful in one way but not another.

Now try this

Jot down what you need to do for
(a) cross-referencing questions. **(b)** usefulness or reliability questions.

Source skills 3

Question 5 carries the highest number of marks so make sure you are prepared.

Question 5: evaluating a hypothesis

The final question gives a hypothesis about a topic – a statement with an opinion.
You must decide if you agree or disagree based on three sources **and** your own knowledge.

You can demonstrate hypothesis evaluation skills by:

☑ carefully reading the statement so you are sure what it is saying

☑ working through sources to decide which ones support the statement and which do not (some might do both)

☑ giving evidence from the sources *and* from your own knowledge

☑ thinking about reliability – how far you trust the source will help you evaluate how much weight you should give to it.

Question 5 is worth 16 marks

• Use the three named sources.

• Find evidence in the sources and from your own knowledge that supports (or not) the hypothesis and reach a conclusion.

• Weigh up the evidence given in the sources with your own knowledge, so you can reach a judgement.

• Use good spelling, grammar and punctuation.

Your own knowledge can be used to add detail to a point given in a source or to explain something not mentioned. You don't need to use much of your own knowledge, but the best answers include some.

Content: what information can you get directly from the source and its caption? It is important to spend time reading and studying sources before you read the exam questions.

Nature: what type of source is it – a diary entry, newspaper article, cartoon? This will help you to assess reliability, purpose and usefulness.

Origins: the caption should tell you who produced the source and when. The origin will help you to assess its reliability, usefulness and purpose.

Bias: a source is still useful even if you think it is biased – it can be good for assessing people's opinions of an event, for example.

Language: in written sources, the author's language should give you clues about whether they are biased or even unreliable. Using appropriate examples by quoting directly from the source will help you gain better marks. Language can also tell you about the purpose of a source.

Hints and tips for examining sources

Purpose: the reason a source was created could be one of the questions by itself, but this will also help you to assess its reliability and usefulness.

Selection: what has the author/artist chosen to include? What have they chosen to leave out? It's important to consider both of these when you are thinking about the reliability, usefulness and purpose of a source.

Now try this

Jot down what you need to do for 'evaluating a hypothesis' questions.

Dealing with pain

Before effective anaesthetics, surgery was very crude and very painful.

Search for an anaesthetic

> Before 1800 alcohol and opium had little success in easing pain during operations.

> Laughing gas was used in 1844 in dentistry in the USA, but failed to ease all pain and patients remained conscious.

> Ether (used from 1846) made patients totally unconscious and lasted a long time. However, it could make patients cough during operations and sick afterwards. It was highly flammable and was transported in heavy glass bottles.

> Chloroform (used from 1847) was very effective with few side effects. However, it was difficult to get the dose right and could kill some people because of the effect on their heart. An inhaler helped to regulate the dosage.

> Cocaine was used as the first local anaesthetic in 1884. In 1905 a less addictive version – novocaine – was used as a general anaesthetic.

Opposition to anaesthetics

People were worried about the long-term effects of using them. Some doctors thought being unconscious made patients more likely to die.

Chloroform use resulted in more complex operations which led to greater blood loss and infection. The number of resulting deaths scared people. Also, the Victorians were very religious and thought that God inflicted pain for a reason, so it was wrong to interfere.

James Simpson

Simpson was the first man to be knighted for services to medicine. He looked for solutions to pain during surgery. He discovered chloroform, then wrote articles and gave lectures to promote its use for surgery and childbirth.

Before anaesthetics	Impact of anaesthetics
Surgery was extremely painful and many patients died from shock.	Surgery became pain free.
Surgeons worked fast to minimise pain and blood loss.	Surgeons could take more time and be more careful though still had to deal with blood loss.
Patients had to be held down, which made it difficult for surgeons.	Patients didn't struggle, so surgeons found operations easier.
Most operations were amputations or close to the surface of the body.	Deeper surgery was possible, increasing the risk of infection. This led to the 'black period' of surgery.

Now try this

What is the purpose of Source A?

How does it try to achieve it?

Source A: *From 'On a new anaesthetic agent, more efficient than sulphuric ether' by James Simpson, writing in the Lancet (a medical journal), 1848.*

As an anaesthetic agent, chloroform possesses, I believe, all the advantages of ether.
- A greatly less quantity is needed to produce the anaesthetic effect.
- Its action is more rapid and complete, and generally more persistent.
- People who have used ether strongly declare it's [chloroform is] far more agreeable and pleasant.

Dealing with infection

Before antiseptics

Many patients died from infections after an operation.

- Surgeons wore clothes covered in dried blood and pus. Some washed their hands, but only with water.
- The places and equipment used for operations were not hygienic.

Joseph Lister

In 1861, Lister became a surgeon at Glasgow Royal Infirmary, where half the patients died from post-operation infections. His experiments led to the development of antiseptics. In 1877, he became Professor of Surgery at King's College Hospital, London, where many surgeons copied his ideas.

Development of antiseptics

After reading Pasteur's germ theory in 1864, Lister learned that carbolic acid killed parasites in sewage.

- In 1865 he soaked bandages in carbolic acid so that a wound did not get infected.
- He used carbolic acid to clean wounds and equipment, and invented a spray to kill germs in the air.
- In 1867, he stated that his wards had been free from sepsis (infections) for nine months, and published his ideas.

Opposition to Lister

Some doctors didn't believe Lister's findings. They found that carbolic acid:
- made their hands sore
- slowed operations down, which led to increased blood loss
- didn't work properly (but this is because they hadn't copied him accurately).

Lister changed his methods to improve them, but some thought he changed them because he was unsure, and that the equipment required was heavy and expensive. Others found that soap and water worked equally well.

Aseptic surgery

By 1890, most operations took place in antiseptic conditions (where antiseptics killed germs). Then aseptic conditions were used (where there would be no germs at all).

Operating theatres and wards were thoroughly cleaned.

Surgeons and nurses wore sterilised clothing.

Sterilised cloths covered surfaces and equipment.

Surgeons and nurses wore masks to prevent breathing infection into a wound.

In 1878, Robert Koch developed a steam steriliser for surgical instruments. After 1887, all surgical equipment was sterilised.

After 1890, anyone touching the patient wore rubber gloves to stop germs passing from their hands to the wound or onto instruments they were using.

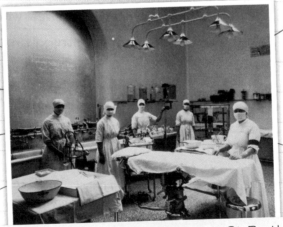

Source B: An operating theatre at St Bartholomew's hospital, London around 1920.

Now try this

To practise your inference skills, jot down things you can learn from Source B about how hospitals were trying to prevent infection by the 1920s.

Dealing with blood loss

Blood loss was a common problem, but early transfusions didn't work. Later experiments meant blood could be stored and correctly used on patients.

Stopping blood flow

A number of methods helped to prevent excess blood loss.

1 **Clamps:** before amputations, clamps or tourniquets stopped blood flowing to the limb about to be amputated. However, this only stopped some of the loss.

2 **Using heat (cautery):** heat from a hot iron rod or hot oil poured on the wound sealed blood vessels. However, it was very painful.

3 **Tying blood vessels:** silk threads (ligatures) tied up the blood vessel. It didn't always succeed but was less painful than cautery.

Silk ligatures could not be sterilised, so using them often led to infection. Joseph Lister introduced sterilised catgut, which prevented infection. He also developed ligatures that dissolved, so there was no need for a thread to be left outside the body to remove the stitches.

EXAM ALERT!

Remember that although they had anaesthetics to deal with pain and antiseptic (or even aseptic) techniques, surgeons could still not risk long and complicated operations where the patient might die from blood loss.

Students have struggled with this topic in recent exams – **be prepared!**

ResultsPlus

Blood transfusions

In the 17th century, doctors did blood transfusions from animals as well as humans. People rarely survived, so it was banned.

⬇

By the late 19th century, safe blood transfusion was needed urgently because of increased surgery.

⬇

In 1901–02, Karl Landsteiner discovered four blood groups. Transfusions would work between people of the same group. However, testing groups and finding donors took too long.

⬇

In 1915, Richard Lewisohn found that adding sodium citrate to blood stopped it clotting, so it could be stored a short time. Richard Weil used refrigerators to store it for much longer.

⬇

In 1916, Francis Rous and James Turner added citrate glucose, which meant blood could be stored even longer.

⬇

Before the Battle of Cambrai in 1917, the army asked the public to donate blood. It was stored in the first blood depot.

Now try this

Jot down at least **two** ways in which Source C would be useful for a historian investigating early blood transfusions and **two** ways in which it wouldn't be useful.

Source C: *A doctor giving a woman a blood transfusion from a volunteer in 1882.*

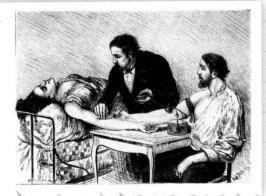

97

Influencing factors

This topic is about the different factors that had an influence on surgery. You will need to learn these factors.

 Science

Science had a positive impact on surgery.

- Anaesthetics developed and improved due to scientific experiments.
- Pasteur's germ theory led to Lister's development of antiseptics.
- Chloroform and blood storage were discovered through chemistry.
- Wilhelm Roentgen discovered X-rays in 1895.

 Technology

Surgery was made easier and safer by technology such as:

- John Snow's chloroform inhaler
- carbolic sprays
- steam sterilisers
- X-ray machines
- Alexander Wood's hypodermic needle.

 Communication

Communication helped spread new ideas and get them accepted. Meetings, newspapers and medical journals helped. For example, Roentgen published his ideas about X-rays and didn't stop people from copying them.

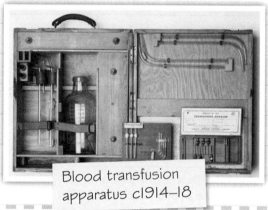

Blood transfusion apparatus c1914–18

 War

The First World War resulted in many different injuries, which required new types of treatment, so it had a big impact on surgery.

- Explosives caused very deep wounds. Field surgeons couldn't carry heavy carbolic acid, so they used saline (salt solution), which worked well.
- Smaller, mobile X-ray machines were developed.
- Prosthetic (false) limbs were improved.
- Facial injuries led Harold Gillies to set up a plastic surgery unit. He developed the work of French surgeon Hippolyte Morestin, keeping careful records and developing new techniques such as skin grafting.

Now try this

To improve your analysis skills, study Source D and jot down how the author tries to communicate their opinion of Gillies' work.

Source D: *From 'Hospital reveals faces of battle' announcing an exhibition on plastic surgery in the First World War in News Shopper, 23 November 2007.*

At this time, most field surgeons stitched the edges of facial wounds together to stop infection, leaving men's faces to become twisted and horribly disfigured as the scar tissue tightened. But Gillies pioneered new treatments, using bone and cartilage, to reconstruct the damaged faces, and a method of growing 'tubes' of the patient's own skin to be used in grafts to help repair injuries. The co-curator of the exhibition, Samantha Doty, says, 'The impact of Gillies' work cannot be underestimated.'

The General Strike

During the General Strike of May 1926, more than 2.5 million workers from many industries went on strike. However, after just nine days the Trades Union Congress (TUC) called off the strike without gaining any concessions.

Main causes

Many causes contributed including:
- long-term tensions in mining
- a post-war industrial slump
- dispute between mine owners and unions over the Samuel Commission's report
- the government called off negotiations with the TUC after workers on the *Daily Mail* refused to print an anti-strike editorial
- unlike during the miners' strikes in 1921, other unions in the Triple Alliance agreed to strike with the miners.

Communism and socialism

There was a communist revolution in Russia in 1917. The Conservative government and non-working classes feared British workers gaining similar power.

Source clues

The British Gazette was the government's newspaper. The *British Worker* was the newspaper of the TUC. This will help you evaluate the reliability and purpose if you come across sources from these newspapers.

Why the strike failed

TUC leaders	Government
Didn't think a general strike would work – tried to negotiate and pressured the Miners' Union to accept the Samuel Commission's report.	Saw the general strike as a huge threat so were determined to end it without giving in to any of the strikers' demands.
The vast majority of TUC leaders were not communists and worried that a general strike would be seen as an attempted revolution.	The government, was united in thinking the strike was an attack on the state itself and 'political' not 'economic'.
TUC leaders weren't allowed to speak on the radio and had limited space in newspapers as the government controlled newsprint.	Had almost total control of the media so the general public only heard what the government wanted them to.
Didn't plan the strike very well. It was more by luck than organisation that the strike was very well supported.	'Red Friday' 1925: Government subsidies delayed miners' wage cuts for 9 months so the government had time to stockpile resources and set up the OMS (Organisation for the Maintenance of Supplies) to train volunteers to replace striking workers.
Felt they were losing control of the strike in some areas and were worried about public opinion if strikers turned to violence.	Used extra police and the army to keep control – their presence on the streets must have been frightening to the general public.

Now try this

Jot down the origin and nature of Source A. Do you think this source is likely to be reliable or not?

Source A: From *A Social and Economic History of Modern Britain* by J. Wilkes, published in 1984.

The Trades Union Congress never used its full strength. Public health workers were deliberately not called out on strike. Strikers all over the country were given strict instructions, which they generally obeyed, to avoid threatening behaviour. TUC leaders wanted to make sure that the strike did not get out of control. The leaders were most certainly not revolutionaries. However, they did know that there were some extremists in the trade union movement. The TUC leaders believed that these extremists wanted the strike to bring down the government.

The miners' strike

The 1984–85 miners' strike lasted 51 weeks before the miners gave up. How did the government 'win'?

Strike triggers

In March 1984, the closure of 20 pits was announced with 20 000 miners losing their jobs. The National Union of Mineworkers began a national strike even though their members were not given a chance to vote for one.

Conservatives vs. trade unions

- The Conservative government had to agree to strikers' demands to end the miners' strikes of 1972 and 1974. It lost power as a result.
- When they were re-elected in 1979, they passed laws reducing the power of the unions, determined not to let them 'win' again.

Source B: Picket line at Ollerton Colliery, Nottinghamshire, 14 March 1984. Yorkshire miner David Jones was killed while picketing.

Tactics of both sides

	Miners	Government
People	Arthur Scargill – leader of the NUM	Margaret Thatcher – Prime Minister
Actions	They 'picketed' mines to prevent other workers from entering. They sometimes fought with police. Flying pickets moved around to strengthen the strike at other pits. Miners who didn't strike were called 'scabs' and badly treated.	It stockpiled coal and converted some power stations to oil. It tried to divide miners by promising some their jobs were safe. It brought in police from around the country to stop the action of 'flying pickets'.
Use of media	They portrayed themselves as fighting for survival against a government determined to destroy their livelihoods. They used the media to describe police intimidation and brutality.	It portrayed miners as a 'mob' using violence against the police and other miners who wanted to work. It fed the media (which was mainly on its side) information about NUM corruption.
Money	They only got financial support from the NUM if they were picketing (to persuade them all to picket). They raised funds using marches, posters and leaflets (many organised by women) plus trade unions abroad.	No vote was held, so the strike was technically 'illegal'. This meant the government could fine the NUM (so it had less money to support the strikers) and not pay strikers any benefits (adding to their struggle).
Other unions	TUC voted to support the miners, but didn't really. Many wouldn't support a strike that hadn't been voted for.	The government managed to get information about the NUM and its plans from other unions.

Now try this

To improve your inference skills, jot down all the things you can learn from Source B about the miners' strike.

Suffragettes

The Women's Social and Political Union (or Suffragettes) was formed in 1903 by a group of former Suffragists (The National Union of Women's Suffrage Societies) led by Emmeline Pankhurst. They had become impatient with the lack of progress made using peaceful protest towards gaining the vote for women.

Suffragette tactics

Giving out leaflets and displaying posters

Suffragette newspaper – The Suffragette

Organising large demonstrations and marches

Publicity stunts

Disrupting political meetings

Breaking windows, damaging property, arson

Chaining themselves to government buildings

Refusing to pay fines after breaking the law so they'd be sent to prison

Hunger strikes while in prison

Emily Davison presented as a martyr

Source C: WSPU poster from 1910

Government responses

As the Suffragette campaigners started to break the law, the Liberal government:

- banned women from Liberal meetings
- classed Suffragette prisoners as criminals rather than political prisoners
- decided to force-feed Suffragette prisoners on hunger strike
- worked with the WSPU and NUWSS on a Conciliation Bill in 1910
- abandoned the Bill, which led to 'Black Friday', when Suffragette protestors were violently treated by the police after the government instructed them to frighten and humiliate Suffragettes
- passed the Cat and Mouse Act in 1913, after public concern over hunger strikers becoming seriously ill. Women were now released and re-arrested when they were better.

The media

Violence and demonstrations by women were shocking. This helped publicise the Suffragettes' aims and put pressure on the government to act. Most newspapers were anti-suffragette but they did get more sympathy when they used peaceful protest or when police used violence.

Were they successful?

In 1918 some women did get the vote. Historians still debate the reasons for this.

- Some claim it was because of the work women did during the First World War.
- Others suggest there was growing support for female suffrage but the Suffragettes damaged their cause because the government wouldn't give in to militancy. The war gave the government an excuse for not saying that the protestors had won.

Now try this

To practise your analysis skills, describe the purpose of Source C above. List ways in which the artist has tried to get their message across.

Poll tax protests

The Community Charge, or 'poll tax', was introduced on 1 April 1989 in Scotland and a year later in England and Wales by the Conservative government. Everyone had to pay the same regardless of their income. This meant that over 70% of the population had to pay more tax.

Who protested?

The Labour Party, trade unions and many people thought the poll tax was unfair. A group called the Anti-Poll Tax Union was set up in Glasgow when the law was announced. Similar groups sprang up throughout Scotland, England and Wales. They distributed information and supported people who didn't pay. They linked together, resulting in the All-Britain Federation, which organised demonstrations. Some led to violence between protestors and police, especially in London on 31 March 1990.

Methods of protest
- Protest marches, petitions and demonstrations
- Information leaflets and posters
- T-shirts, stickers, badges and mugs with anti-poll tax slogans
- Not registering for the new tax
- Refusing to pay the new tax
- People in local councils not administering or collecting the tax

Government responses

This was a new type of protest, and the government found it difficult to cope with.

- Margaret Thatcher and other Conservatives presented protesters as 'rent-a-mob', but only a few protestors were violent. The protestors generally had public opinion on their side.
- Because protests began in local communities, there were no national leaders who the government could negotiate with.
- Not paying taxes is against the law but the government couldn't arrest 18 million people!
- The government lost more support as heavy-handed policing made it look as if they had lost control (rather than protestors being at fault).

There is no doubt that poll tax protests were successful as the tax was ended and Mrs Thatcher was forced to resign shortly after.

Now try this

Jot down **two** ways in which Source D would be **useful** to a historian looking at methods used by the poll tax protestors and **two** ways in which it wouldn't be useful.

Source D: *From an article by Tommy Sheridan, one of the leaders of the poll tax protests in Scotland, written in 2009.*

The Government had ignored petitions, protest marches, rallies and people's votes. All we had left was the right to protest through civil disobedience and mass non-payment of the Poll Tax. By the end of 1989, nearly a million people were not paying the tax. Marches and rallies involved tens of thousands of people. Council buildings were occupied. Officials sent to enforce the charge were stopped from entering non-payers' homes and often returned to find their own offices under siege. The tax was further weakened when the campaign spread to England and Wales; 13 million new non-payers made the Poll Tax a dead duck.

Answers

UNIT 1A: MEDICINE

1 Medicine in c1350

Reasons include the following:

People believed Galen was totally correct, so they accepted his ideas.

Questioning and experimenting was not encouraged by the authorities.

Christianity was the dominant force and the Church liked and accepted Galen's ideas.

The Church disapproved of dissection, so people didn't check Galen's theories for themselves.

Few other plausible theories had come along.

The number of books Galen wrote meant that his ideas were dominant.

2 Treating the sick c1350

Factors include the following:

Cost: physicians were very expensive.

Availability: there were not many physicians and they were mainly in towns; people were most likely to use a housewife physician or apothecary.

Training: physicians were the best trained, so were more respected. People would have used them if they could have afforded it.

Type of illness or injury: barber surgeons might have been visited for bloodletting, pulling teeth, etc.; apothecaries for remedies; hospitals for specific diseases like leprosy.

3 The Black Death

Examples of causes and corresponding ways of prevention include the following:

If people believed the Black Death was caused by God as a punishment for sins, they might pray or fast; flagellants walked in a procession to a church whipping themselves and praying.

If they believed it was caused by miasma, they might clean up the rubbish in their homes or on the streets, carry herbs and spices to stop them breathing in the bad air, and try to keep the air moving by flying birds or lighting a fire.

If they believed it was caused by poisonous gases from volcanoes and earthquakes, they might light fires and try to keep the air moving in rooms; they might carry herbs and spices near their noses and mouths to avoid breathing in bad air.

If they believed it was caused by outsiders, they might try to stop strangers entering their village or at least their homes.

4 The Renaissance

(a) Things that changed were:

The rise of science led people to question beliefs.

Ideas about anatomy were improved as people began carrying out dissections, e.g. Vesalius.

Ideas about the circulation of the blood were improved by Harvey.

Improvements in communications (e.g. the printing press) meant that ideas began to spread more easily.

New and improved technology (e.g. improved microscopes) had an effect on science and medicine.

(b) Things that stayed the same were:

Training for doctors was still based on Galen's theories.

Understanding of the causes of disease didn't change, so neither did treatment nor prevention.

5 Industrialisation

Reasons include:

Little fresh food in towns and cities, which meant people were more susceptible to catching diseases such as TB.

Urban growth and overcrowding in towns and cities (especially in poor areas), which meant that disease spread very quickly.

Contaminated water, which caused many infectious diseases such as cholera and typhoid; more drinking water was contaminated due to pollution in overcrowded towns and poor public health provision.

6 Breakthroughs, 1750–1900

Factors include:

Jenner as an individual; the way he worked and the fact that he used scientific methods and thinking.

Communication, which meant other people heard about his ideas (he published his own results).

The work of the Jennerian Society to promote vaccination.

People accepting the theory and being prepared to be vaccinated.

Government action in making vaccination compulsory.

7 Professionalising medicine

Factors include:

Introduction of teaching hospitals, where students could receive practical training and learn from other doctors.

Scientific approaches to medicine.

The introduction of examinations and registration.

Improved knowledge of anatomy through dissection.

Improved technology which helped diagnose some illnesses.

8 Treatment, 1750–1900

Examples include:

Hospitals were cleaner and more hygienic so infection was less likely.

Nurses were trained and had a more central role, so they gave better care.

Hospitals were better designed in terms of light, ventilation and sanitation.

Visitors were no longer involved in caring for the patients.

Public pressure led to infirmaries (separate from workhouses) for the poorest people in society.

Specialist hospitals for different conditions meant that infectious people were kept separate from others and patients were more likely to receive specialist care.

9 Causes of disease since 1900

Reasons include:

The discovery of the structure of DNA led to a greater understanding of genetic conditions and a realisation that some illnesses (such as some types of cancer) could have a genetic cause.

The discovery of stem cells has led to the possibility of replacing faulty cells.

It led to better vaccines for some conditions.

New techniques for skin grafts.

It is used to create cells that can manufacture insulin and help diabetes sufferers.

10 Treatment since 1900

(a) Factors that led to the development of magic bullets include:

scientific research

technology (e.g. microscopes)

government funding

luck or chance

communication

team work.

(b) Factors that led to penicillin as a cure include:

scientific research

luck or chance

war

communication

government funding

perseverance of individuals

team work.

11 Health care since 1900 (1)

Reasons include:

They couldn't afford a doctor who would prescribe more scientific treatment.

They couldn't afford the treatment itself.

There were few doctors in poor areas.

They didn't trust science or know about the medical developments.

12 Health care since 1900 (2)

Reasons include:

Improved living conditions.

Increase in wealth – people eating better, etc.

Government funding of health care.

Better education, helping people to lead healthier lives.

Better understanding of what causes disease.

Increased prevention of diseases through vaccination.

Scientific breakthroughs in chemical cures, antibiotics, blood transfusions and other treatments.

Improved technology to diagnose, monitor and treat illness.

Improved and more professional training of doctors, nurses and paramedics.

13 Medicine in Roman Britain

Examples include:

The public health system was good.

There was little effort to find out what caused disease.

People were happy to continue to accept Greek ideas.

No new treatments for disease developed under the Romans – they were happy to use Greek ideas or the remedies of the local population.

There wasn't any training for doctors and they weren't really respected.

14 Public health in Roman Britain

Reasons include:

The Romans believed there was a link between dirt and disease, so wanted to keep themselves and where they lived as clean as they could.

It was a wealthy society so people and the government could afford to pay to build and maintain public health facilities.

The government was strong so could enforce its will in keeping towns clean.

Public baths were central to the social lives of Romans as well as to public health.

Roman engineers and builders had the knowledge needed to build public health facilities.

The army and slaves provided the workers to build and maintain public health facilities.

15 Continuity c43 to c1350

These include:

Most people were treated by family members.

There were few doctors.

Ideas about the cause of and cures for disease remained the same – supernatural or religious causes, use of herbal remedies.

Treatment based on getting rid of excess humours – bloodletting, purging, etc.

Reliance on Galen's theories and treatments.

16 Medieval medicine

(a) Ways it helped:

It emphasised caring for the sick and set up hospitals.

It maintained libraries of books containing medical teachings.

It developed centres of learning.

(b) Ways it hindered:

It didn't approve of people questioning their traditional beliefs and ideas about the causes of disease.

The emphasis was on caring for the sick, not on curing disease.

It made sure the focus was on religion – both as a cause and possible cure for disease.

17 Medieval public health

Reasons include:

There was more war and conflict in society after the Romans left, so governments were focused on winning battles and keeping power rather than setting up and maintaining public health systems.

Roman government had all the power; medieval governments had to share power with the Church.

Roman governments were wealthier than Saxon monarchs.

Later medieval towns and cities were bigger and therefore public health problems were worse.

18 Public health: problems, 1350–1750

Examples include:

Infectious diseases spread faster.

It caused disease and infection, especially through contaminated water and poor sanitation.

Rubbish, dead animals and excrement left on the streets could cause disease.

19 Public health: action, 1350–1900

Reasons include:

Lack of understanding of the real causes of disease meant actions often weren't successful.

Public attitudes – people didn't want the government involved in their lives and health.

People still thought God caused disease.

Lack of money because governments weren't prepared to raise taxes to fund public health provision.

20 Industrial diseases

Reasons include:

They didn't believe the government should interfere in people's lives.

They thought it was unfair that the changes would be paid for by people who would not benefit from them – through taxes on the middle and upper classes.

The belief that the government shouldn't interfere in private businesses – water was supplied by private companies, private companies removed sewage, etc.

21 Government action

Chadwick was influential because:

His report brought problems to people's attention.

He helped to set up the Public Health Act of 1848 and he was a commissioner on the General Board of Health which was set up as a result.

Chadwick made little difference because:

Little was actually done that he suggested.

The changes made under the Public Health Act were short-lived.

The Public Health Act didn't enforce change so most town councils didn't do anything.

22 Public health since 1900

Factors include:

Attitudes: for example in allowing more government intervention in private lives.

Government: several governments have been willing to make changes.

War: led to changes in attitudes and the role of government, and heightened awareness of health inequalities.

Science: led to new vaccines, etc.

Laws: improved sewerage systems, etc.

Education: more awareness of health issues and what causes disease.

UNIT 1B: CRIME

23 Crime and punishment in 1450

Lawmakers made punishment harsh to try to deter people from committing what they regarded as serious crimes and protect their power and property.

Punishments were usually given in public, so they involved humiliation.

Criminals were removed from society (by the death penalty) to make society better.

24 Crime, 1450–1750

Crimes that did not increase, and stayed the same:

theft
rape
burglary
murder
assault

Crimes that increased, or new crimes that developed:

begging/vagrancy
smuggling goods
highway robbery
heresy
treason
poaching

25 Begging and treason

(a) Reasons why begging became a crime:

No system to help the needy, and people resented paying to support them, which meant begging increased.

Society felt threatened by the increase in the number of 'unknown' beggars in towns.

Theft and street crime was increasing at the same time – thought to be caused by beggars.

(b) Reasons why charges of treason became more common between 1450 and 1750:

There were more plots against monarchs because of political and religious changes.

Rulers felt insecure and therefore the charge of treason was used more to deter people from committing treason.

Some rulers used treason as an excuse for getting rid of people who crossed them.

26 Punishment, 1450–1750

Aims include:

Deterrence: to stop others from committing crime, either through fear (of corporal or capital punishment) or through humiliation (being put in the stocks or pillory).

Retribution: to punish people harshly for doing wrong.

Protecting society: by removing criminals either through death or, later in the period, transportation.

27 Crime, 1750–1900 (1)

They were likely to commit prostitution, theft (especially of food) burglary, poaching (for food), and drunk and disorderly behaviour. They could also be led into a criminal gang working professionally.

28 Crime, 1750–1900 (2)

Reasons include:

Customs officers couldn't patrol all of the coast, which was a huge area.

The general public largely supported the smugglers (they thought they were heroes); therefore, they hid them or provided them with alibis. People also hid, traded and bought the goods that smugglers brought into Britain.

29 Policing, 1750–1900

Reasons include:

The police were now well trained, so knew how to do a good job in preventing and detecting crime.

Their work was full time and they were well paid, so they wanted to do a good job.

They won the trust of the general public which helped the police solve crimes.

Uniformed police patrolling areas of high street crime stopped people from committing crime.

30 Punishment, 1750–1900

Hanging was seen as too harsh for petty crime, so alternatives were looked for. Transportation was used as an alternative, but this began to be seen as too harsh a punishment as well. It was too expensive and Australia didn't want more criminals. There was an increase in prisons, and imprisonment was now seen as an acceptable form of punishment. Some started thinking that punishment should also be about reforming people (shown in Peel's prison reforms).

31 Crime since 1900 (1)

(a) Traffic crime: invention of modern transport meant that driving offences/traffic crimes such as speeding, driving dangerously, driving under the influence of alcohol, etc., plus car theft, have become crimes.

(b) Race crime: Britain deveoped into a society that was multicultural, with people of different races and religions – racism was seen as being a crime which should therefore be punished.

32 Crime since 1900 (2)

(a) Modern 'social crimes' include: smuggling of legal goods without paying tax; tax evasion.

(b) Genuinely 'new' crimes include: driving offences; computer hacking; race crimes.

(b) 'New' crimes that are actually 'old' crimes using modern technology include: fraud using computer technology; identity theft; car theft (horse theft before!); terrorism (using modern weapons and technology).

33 Policing since 1900

Fingerprinting: helps to catch and prosecute criminals, as fingerprints found at the scene can only belong to one person. Databases shared between police forces help to identify people from their fingerprints.

Radios: make it easier for police to report problems and request help if needed.

Computers: used for preventing crime through monitoring electronic communication and used for catching and prosecuting people as police can sort through huge amounts of information in databases.

DNA evidence: like fingerprints, can be used to identify criminals (and victims) from hair, skin or blood found at the scene of a crime.

Cars, motorbikes, helicopters: allow police to get to crime scenes very quickly and chase criminals if necessary.

CCTV: can be used for both prevention (people are deterred from committing crime if they think CCTV is being used) and for identifying and catching criminals once a crime has been committed.

34 Punishment since 1900

Punishment/retribution: to punish someone by depriving them of their freedom.

Deterrence: to deter/try to stop people from committing crime.

To keep society safe by removing criminals.

Restitution: people who have done wrong do something for society through unpaid work.

Reform: to change the person so they won't commit more crime when they are released back into society.

35 Continuity and change

Reasons include:

Punishment was at its harshest when 'foreigners' ruled in Roman times and after the Norman invasion to try to keep order and prevent rebellion.

Punishments became slightly more lenient after the Romans left because of the influence of the Church – idea of reforming the sinner.

Stability of the ruler – resulting in better law enforcement and less crime.

36 Roman Britain

Examples include:

One central system of law and law enforcement.

Laws publicly displayed, so everyone knew what they were.

Suspects thought of as innocent until proven otherwise, but, if guilty, were punished according to whether they were men, women, citizens, non-citizens or slaves (slaves often not punished as harshly because they were needed by their owners).

Crime against authority/those in charge received harshest punishment.

37 Anglo-Saxon England

(a) 'Similar' examples:

Types of crime committed were mostly the same

Most punishments continued to be used.

The most powerful made the laws.

(b) 'Different' examples:

Anglo-Saxon families and communities were responsible for law enforcement (rather than the Roman army).

Capital punishment was used far less frequently.

Influence of the Church meant more mutilations were given instead of the death penalty.

The Church also made some new laws.

Different laws in each kingdom.

Use of wergeld or compensation was new.

Trial by ordeal was introduced.

38 Norman England

Similarities include:

Many laws were the same as during Anglo-Saxon times.

Power of the king was still important in enforcing the law (actually became more important).

Systems of enforcing the law – tithings, hue and cry, trial by jury in courts – were the same.

The Church was still important (became more important).

39 Later Medieval England

Differences include:

Posses formed to help sheriffs chase and catch criminals.

County gaols kept people for trial.

Royal courts dealt with serious crimes under common law.

Justices of the Peace, appointed by the king, acted as judges in county courts.

40 Witchcraft 1

Examples include the following:

After Elizabeth I came to power: the new law defined major and minor witchcraft clearly so it became easier to prosecute people. It was a time of plots and conspiracies, so the authorities and people generally were more suspicious.

During reign of James I: he was very concerned about witchcraft and encouraged prosecutions. It was a time of many plots and conspiracies against the king, so people were more suspicious.

During English Civil War: society was hugely disrupted and tensions heightened; people looked for someone to blame for the terrible things that were happening; the Civil War caused great economic hardship which fostered bad feeling in communities; more people travelled around so there were more strangers in communities; more women were left alone as men went off to fight.

41 Witchcraft 2

Reasons include:

Peace meant tensions in communities eased.

Society became more prosperous, so fewer people looking for a scapegoat.

Authorities were less concerned with witchcraft, so didn't enforce the law as much (witchcraft laws were abolished in 1736).

Superstition was dying out (especially in towns and cities).

Science began to offer good explanations for things previously thought to be the work of witches.

42 Conscientious objection

Reasons include:

Memories of the First World War meant that more people were anti-war, and many more people refused to fight in the Second World War.

Government attitudes had changed, so conscientious objectors were less likely to be imprisoned.

Government made more effort to find COs jobs supporting the war effort but not fighting.

Tribunals were 'fairer' because they were not conducted by the military groups.

Organisations supported COs more and encouraged people not to fight.

43 Domestic violence 1

Reasons include:

Attitudes in the law lagged behind those of public opinion (e.g. incidents of domestic violence were socially condemned in the 19th century).

Women campaigned for rights, but did not receive the vote on equal terms with men until 1928.

Belief that the law shouldn't interfere in people's private lives.

Laws were generally made by men.

In the 19th century, domestic violence was generally associated with the working classes and alcohol; middle-class domestic violence was 'invisible'.

Many women were too scared to make complaints against violent husbands.

44 Domestic violence 2

Factors include the following:

Campaign groups: tried to highlight the suffering caused by domestic violence to change opinions of the authorities; used protest marches and rallies to gain publicity; Erin Pizzey opened Chiswick Women's Aid and highlighted the need for shelters/protection for female victims of domestic abuse. Women's liberation groups raised public awareness to improve women's rights and equality in the law.

New state roles: it was accepted that the state should interfere in private lives to protect children.

Female political power: women's votes became increasingly important to MPs so they began to consider more women's issues, and some female (and male) MPs began to raise the subject in Parliament.
The media: raised awareness by covering domestic violence stories in the news and giving campaign groups publicity.

UNIT 2B: AMERICAN WEST

In order to fully answer some of the questions you will find it useful to have a good knowledge of the whole unit.

45 Life on the Plains
Ways include:
For food.
For clothing and equipment (for example, tipis, tools, ornaments, dung for fuel, soap, blankets, food bags, buckets, cooking pots, drinking vessels, knives, glue, shields, horse harnesses).
In spiritual/religious rituals (e.g. leaving the animal's heart on the plain to give new life to a herd).

46 Indian society
Examples include the following:
The very old or young who were too frail to travel would be left to die so the rest of the band could follow the buffalo.
Braves could have more than one wife to make sure that as many children as possible were produced for the survival of the band.
Decisions were taken by band councils consulting with their warrior societies.
Fighting for a cause or to the death was seen as selfish, as that brave would no longer be able to hunt and help the band survive.
Everyone in the band was responsible for bringing up children to ensure skills and knowledge were passed on.

47 Why move west?
Farmers: wheat prices had crashed in the economic depression, so many farmers had to sell their farms. Land in the west was 'free' and fertile, so they hoped to be able to set up successful farms there. The government act of 1842 made land in Oregon cheap, which would have been another pull factor for farmers with little money.
Mormons: persecution, though some may have moved for economic reasons as well. They would have been attracted by spacious land, free from persecutors.
Unemployed workers: jobs were hard to find because of the economic depression, so many moved west to set up their own farms or find jobs in the new towns that were emerging or find gold and get rich quick.
Failed businessmen: they had suffered in the economic depression, so the West provided new opportunities for them – such as finding and mining gold, setting up their own farms, and setting up new businesses in the towns that were emerging.

48 The journey west

Danger	How people could prepare for it
Getting lost or stuck	Early migrants used a mountain man or Indian guide; later ones used pamphlets and maps created by mountain men. Sticking to the known routes and trails. Taking equipment to help dig out, repair and haul wagons.
Starvation	Taking as much food and livestock as possible. Making sure the party included hunters who could hunt in all types of terrain (plains, desert, mountains etc.).
Climate	Taking clothing to protect against the cold and desert sun. Avoiding the mountains in the winter months.
Rough terrain	Taking the correct equipment – ropes, pulleys, etc., to get over the mountains.
Hostile Indians	Having an Indian in the travelling party (might not work depending on which tribe they were from). Befriending and trading with Indians encountered on the journey.
Stampeding buffalo	Not much you could do except travel at the times of year when buffalo were least likely to be in that area.
Injury	Most injuries were caused by accidents involving wagons, so using the advice above and not getting into trouble was best. If possible, taking someone in the party who had medical knowledge.

49 The Gold Rush
Differences include the following:
Motivations of gold migrants were more likely to be purely financial.
Early gold miners (mostly male) were not permanent migrants – they just wanted to get rich and go home again.
Gold migrants were far more diverse than other types of migrant and included Europeans and Asians – anyone who wanted to get rich.
Some gold miners were backed by businessmen.

50 The Mormons
Reasons include:
Brigham Young's decisions and organisational skills.
There wasn't the same 'land grab' as in other places, as land was owned by the Church and allocated to families.
Towns were well planned.
A good irrigation system meant that farmland got the water it needed to prosper.
Different skilled people were selected to live in different places, so there was a good mix of skills in each place.
Their faith, which prevented them giving up in the face of terrible hardship.
The Perpetual Emigration Fund helped to bring thousands more Mormons with skills needed for each town.
There were few non-Mormons to persecute them, as had happened elsewhere.
The choice of the Great Salt Lake meant few other migrants wanted to take the land there.
Highly disciplined, religious group who all followed their leader.
Many of these reasons could be seen as the most important, so make sure that you justify your choice.

51 Settling the Plains
Reasons include:
The government believed it was white Americans' 'Manifest Destiny' to inhabit all of the North American continent.
The government believed getting white Americans to live on the Plains made them more secure (it made it less likely that foreign powers such as Mexico and France would try to take the Plains back).
It would increase the prosperity of the USA by allowing more food and goods to be produced.
It would help to solve some of the problems in the Eastern States, such as overcrowding and economic problems.
All of California and Oregon had been settled by 1860, so the Great Plains were the only place left.

52 Farming the Plains
Ways include:
Helping to build the sod houses.
Collecting dung for fuel.
Growing vegetables and helping on the farm.
Caring for the sick using their own remedies.
Helping to raise and educate children.
Building relationships with other farms.
Teaching in schools (done by single women who were brought in specially).

53 The importance of railroads
Reasons include:
More railroads meant more journeys that people could make on the trains, therefore making the railroad companies more money in the long term.
More railroads meant businesses could pay the railroad companies to transport raw materials and goods across larger areas, again making the railroad companies more money in the long term.
Some railroads would transport goods to ports that were well positioned to trade with the Far East.
The huge amounts of money needed to be paid out in order to build the railroads was reduced by the government giving the companies the land to build on (so they only had to spend on workers, materials, etc. and not on land), and they could borrow against or sell the land to raise more money.
The shareholders of railroad companies may have wanted to build more railroads to increase trade (they may have had shares in other companies), and they might have believed that more railroads would help to achieve the nation's Manifest Destiny.

54 The impact of railroads
Ways include:
Railroads made it easier for families and their property to move onto the Plains.
Railroads meant that homesteaders could buy farm machinery such as wind pumps and drills, barbed wire, ploughs, reapers, threshers and binders that made farming the Plains easier and meant that more crops could be produced.
Railroads meant that more markets were available for the crops that homesteaders produced – they could be sold in towns and cities thousands of miles away, which made farming more profitable.
Railroads brought other goods and services such as furniture, oil lamps, clothes and shoes, which made living on the Plains easier.
Railroads increased the size and number of towns, meaning that more services such as churches, doctors and schools were within reach of many homesteads.
Railroads made it easier to keep in contact with other people or visit them, making life less lonely.

55 Cattle trails
Reasons include:

The Civil War meant that cattle herds in Texas had grown massively, so there was plenty of beef available.

Railroads opened up new markets for buying beef, as cattle could be transported to the eastern cities.

The increasing prosperity of Americans meant that more people could afford to buy beef regularly.

The development of cow towns meant that it became easier to buy and sell cattle.

56 Cattle ranches
(See also page 55 in your preparation for this answer.)

Charles Goodnight: a Texan cattleman who established a cattle trail – the Goodnight-Loving Trail. This didn't go to a railhead though. Instead, it went to Fort Sumner where Goodnight supplied beef to the army and nearby Indian reservation. He then made a large profit.

Joseph McCoy: founded the first cow town – Abilene. Cow towns were his idea. Abilene made him lots of money. Other men followed his example and set up more cow towns.

John Iliff: an entrepreneur who set up the first large cattle ranch on the Plains. Other cattlemen followed suit. He also experimented with breeding cattle for better tasting beef, won contracts to supply railroad construction workers and a tribe of Sioux Indians, and used refrigerated railroad cars to transport beef to the eastern states.

57 Cowboys
Reasons include:

The cattle industry itself changed: driving cattle huge distances to railheads and cow towns was dangerous because of the weather, stampeding cattle, and the risk of drowning in rivers or quicksand, wild animals, hostile Indians, cattle rustlers, etc. Drives were replaced by ranches on the plains.

Technology such as barbed wire and refrigerated cars on trains meant that trails were no longer necessary, as ranches could be used.

Ranches meant cattle were better fed, so the meat produced was better and allowed for experiments in breeding. As ranches became smaller after the bust, fewer cowboys were needed so some lost their jobs and had to find other work.

58 Law and order 1
(See also page 59 in your preparation for this answer.)

Reasons include:

Mainly male population (including criminals and ex-soldiers).

Cow towns grew so fast that law enforcement couldn't keep up.

There was conflict between the different groups there.

They were far away from the federal government in Washington.

They were places where huge numbers of cowboys descended at the same time.

Cowboys let off steam in cow towns after long drives.

Most cowboys carried guns; few respected the law.

They were places where large amounts of money changed hands.

There were lots of saloons so people got drunk.

Some law enforcers were corrupt.

59 Law and order 2
(Other topics in this unit may help you with your answer to this question.)

Ways include:

They appointed US marshals and deputy marshals who were responsible for law and order in territories and towns.

They appointed judges to tour the West and try criminals in federal courts.

They helped to bring the railroads to the West, which meant it was easier for law enforcers to reach the towns.

They encouraged migration to the West. Increased population meant the territories could become states which could employ their own law enforcement officers. More families settled in the West who wanted to live in safe towns where the law was enforced.

60 Permanent Indian Frontier
(Other topics in this unit may help you with your answer to this question.)

Reasons include:

The US government couldn't stop individual white Americans from moving across the Indian Frontier.

The government wanted white Americans to spread across the whole country to protect it from foreign powers.

The idea of Manifest Destiny.

The government wanted minerals (especially gold) for US economy.

It wanted land for homesteaders and cattle ranchers – again to strengthen the country and the economy.

Government broke its promises when it found uses for land that had been given to Indians.

A series of treaties was needed for different tribes, so it became hard to enforce all of them.

61 The Indian Wars
(a) Little Crow's War: starvation on the reservation (crops failed and food promised by the government didn't arrive).

(b) Sand Creek Massacre: starvation on the reservation (crops failed; they stole food from wagon trains they had attacked, but didn't harm travellers).

(c) Red Cloud's War: Bozeman Trail and US army forts being built on Sioux land (this broke the first Fort Laramie Treaty 1851).

62 The Great Sioux War
Reasons include:

General Custer and his men were killed, which showed Indian strength.

The shocking massacre changed public opinion among white Americans towards Indians.

It changed US government policy towards Indians.

'Victory' for the Indians actually led to their defeat; they were pursued until forced onto reservations where they had to sell their land and live under military rule.

63 Role of the army
Reasons include:

They trained to fight major battles until death if necessary.

They carried rifles and ammunition; had access to other guns.

They recruited spies from tribes that were hostile to other tribes.

They fought as a unit, with set tactics.

They were based in forts along trails and near reservations, which gave them safe places close to Indian territory.

They fought against the whole tribe (women, the elderly, children and animals).

They attacked Indians during winter, when they were vulnerable (the army had good shelter and food).

All the reasons were important and it was the combination of factors that led to Indians' military defeat. However, a case could be made for each reason being seen as most important. Make sure that you explain your choice.

64 Role of government
Reasons include:

Belief in Manifest Destiny.

It thought settling the whole of the US would make the country more secure.

It wanted to make the US wealthy.

Racism.

Fear of Indian attacks and their unchristian way of life.

Indians couldn't vote – only white Americans could elect the government so the government naturally wanted to please white Americans.

65 Reservations
Ways include:

Plains Indians were used to roaming across vast areas; reservations meant they had to stay in one place.

They couldn't hunt buffalo or make clothes, tipis, etc., out of the buffalo.

Reservations encouraged Indians to farm the land – most hadn't done so before.

Religious/spiritual ceremonies were banned.

Children were taken away and educated, rather than taught the Indian way of life from their parents and elders.

Chiefs lost their power.

Epidemics such as measles and 'flu were rife.

Living conditions were poor.

Their horses were taken away from them.

66 Destruction of the buffalo
Examples include:

Hunting for sport.

Hunting to make way for railroads.

Hunting to feed railroad workers.

Hunting to sell buffalo hides to make goods.

Destroying their habitat by building on the land.

Bringing cattle onto the Plains, which brought diseases that killed buffalo.

Cattle and horses competed with the buffalo for grass and usually won because they were fenced in.

67 End of Indian resistance
(Other topics in this unit may help you with your answer to this question.)

Long-term causes:

Destruction of the buffalo: loss of Indians' food supply, made them dependent on reservations.

Railroads: brought migrants, tourists and soldiers to the Plains.

Government reservation policies: to 'civilise' Indians – turn them into farmers and Christians.

Cultural differences: meant white men feared Indians.

Cattle trails and ranching: took up Indian lands; competed with buffalo.

Homesteads on the Plains: took up Indian lands; fenced land off so hunting was harder.

Short-term causes:

Failed harvests led to starvation.

US army actions: killed Indians; destroyed their property; arrested leaders.

Discovery of gold: brought thousands of miners onto Indians' sacred land.

UNIT 2C: GERMANY

In order to fully answer some of the questions you will find it useful to have a good knowledge of the whole unit.

68 The Weimar Republic, 1919–22

Reasons include:
Many Germans didn't believe Germany had lost the war at all.
They saw the Treaty as 'dictated' rather than negotiated.
They felt the payment of reparations was harsh.
Having to admit blame for starting the war was seen by many Germans as the worst thing about the Treaty at the time.
They resented loss of territory.
Reductions in army and navy, and demilitarisation of the Rhineland, left some Germans feeling vulnerable and reduced Germany's standing as a great power.

69 Opposition groups, 1919–22

Nationalism: belief in the greatness of Germany; hatred of Treaty of Versailles.
Socialism: wanted workers to get a share of company's profits, and land to be shared out more.
Anti-communism: hatred of Russia and of the German Communist Party, which they associated with Jews and Slavs (seen as inferior races). Against communist ideals of destroying private enterprise and property.
Anti-semitism: hatred of Jews and the belief that they were the cause of Germany's problems.

70 Hyperinflation, 1923

Ways include the following:
Pensions became worthless. Those affected included the elderly and war widows.
Savings became worthless. Those affected included probably the middle-classes because they had savings. However, people with mortgages and loans benefitted as they could pay them off. Businesses with loans also benefitted, and some of these businesses took over struggling businesses.
Fixed rents became cheaper. Those affected included people who rented rooms or shops.
Day-to-day life became harder and unpredictable for everyone – prices might change by the time you got to the shop, etc. Those affected included everyone, but particularly the less well off.
Wages didn't rise as quickly. Those affected included workers.
Higher price of food. Those affected included farmers, because they were paid higher sums for their products.
Price of raw materials, parts, etc., rose. Those affected included some businesses, which went bankrupt.

71 Munich Putsch, 1923

Can be seen as a failure because:
The aims of taking over Bavarian government weren't achieved.
The Nazi Party was banned.
Hitler and others put in prison
The people of Munich/army/police didn't support the Nazis.

Can be seen as a success because:
The Nazis reorganised and rethought their strategy for taking power.
They gained huge publicity from Hitler's trial, and Hitler had time to write *Mein Kampf*.
The people were sympathetic to Nazi ideas – the Party was only banned for a short time and Hitler given a very lenient sentence.

72 Weimar recovery, 1924–29

Policies include:
The end of passive resistance and agreement to pay reparations, which led to the French withdrawing from the Ruhr.
The introduction of the Rentenmark, which stabilised German currency and ended hyperinflation.
Negotiation of the Dawes and Young Plans and Locarno Treaties.
Negotiation of the German entry into League of Nations, which improved Germany's standing in the world.

73 The Nazi Party, 1924–28

Reasons include:
Messages were kept simple.
Propaganda was targeted at different groups.
Speakers were trained to get the message across at meetings.
Military-style rallies were effective ways of showing strength and gaining support, particularly among the young.
Mein Kampf became a bestseller after the publicity from Hitler's trial.

74 The Great Depression

Differences include:
The Depression was international (hyperinflation just affected Germany), which meant other countries couldn't help Germany.
Prices didn't rise hugely, as they had with hyperinflation.
Hyperinflation benefited some German people – very few benefited from the Great Depression.
Unemployment was much worse in the Great Depression and more businesses went bust.

75 The Nazi Party, 1929–32

Reasons include:
Fear of communism.
They agreed with anti-semitic policies.
Unemployment.
The Weimar government was unable to sort out the problems of the Depression.
Persuaded by the propaganda spreading Nazi ideas; this was everywhere – posters, radio, newspapers, etc.
People thought Hitler was the strong leader Germany needed to get them out of trouble.

76 Hitler becomes Chancellor

Reasons include:
Hindenburg appointed him.
Von Papen persuaded Hindenburg to appoint him.
In July 1932 and November 1932 the Nazi Party got the most votes (were the largest party in the Reichstag).
Von Schleicher resigned and Hindenburg didn't have a choice.
Hindenburg and von Papen thought they'd be able to control Hitler.

77 Key events, 1933

Reasons include:
The Enabling Act meant Hitler didn't need the support of the Reichstag for four years.
It allowed Hitler to make whatever laws the Nazis wanted.
It led to the abolition of state parliaments.
It led to the abolition of trade unions.
It led to the abolition of other political parties – reducing the power of everyone except the Nazis (and Hindenburg).

78 Key events, 1934

Reasons include:
The Enabling Act meant that Hitler could remove political opponents – state parliaments, trade unions and other political parties.
The Night of the Long Knives removed the SA and other political opponents.
The Night of the Long Knives meant the army swore allegiance to Hitler.
The death of Hindenburg meant Germany no longer had a President; Hitler combined this role with Chancellor to become Führer.

79 Nazi use of terror

Ways include:
They had unlimited powers to arrest people and imprison them without trial.
The mere presence/threat of SS was terrifying.
They were supported by the Gestapo, block wardens and spies.
They ran the concentration and death camps.

80 Censorship and propaganda

Ways include:
- posters
- films in the cinema
- parades
- school books
- plays
- music.
- radio programmes
- marches
- through youth organisations
- rallies
- art

81 The Churches

Ways include:
Catholic Concordat, which gave Catholics the freedom to worship in return for staying out of politics.
Reich Church, set up for Protestants.
Churchmen/priests who disagreed with the Nazis were sent to concentration camps.
Catholic schools were closed and youth organisations made illegal.

82 Opposition 1

Examples include:
Martin Niemöller set up the Confessional Church in opposition to the Reich Church.
Priests and ministers spoke out and preached against the Nazi regime.
Cardinal Galen spoke out about the T4 euthanasia programme in 1938, and it was ended.
Dietrich Bonhoeffer plotted to overthrow Hitler.
Some hid Jews and/or helped them to escape.
Some classed going to church itself as an act of opposition, as the Nazis were opposed to religion.

83 Opposition 2

Types of opposition include:
Speaking out publicly against Nazi policies (e.g. Pastor Niemöller and other church ministers).
Helping or hiding Jews (e.g. Dietrich Bonhoeffer).
Distributing anonymous leaflets publicising Nazi atrocities (e.g. White Rose Group).

Refusing to **attend** Nazi Youth organisations (e.g. Edelweiss Pirates).
Spreading **Allied** propaganda (e.g. Edelweiss Pirates).
Trying to **kill** Hitler (e.g. Count von Stauffenberg and other army officers).

84 Policies towards women

The source **is** from the official Nazi magazine for women, so they would show their 'ideal' **woman** on the cover. She has three children, which implies that the Nazis **thought** having children and looking after them was what women should do. The woman **and** children are all Aryan, with blond hair and blue eyes. This shows that the **Nazis** thought women were important for producing pure Aryan Germans. The woman **is** not glamorous, showing how the Nazis preferred women to be strong, **healthy** and practical.

85 Nazi education

Reasons **include:**
It would **make** the 'future' (children) of Germany loyal Nazis.
It would **prepare** boys to be soldiers and workers.
It would **prepare** girls to be wives and mothers.
It would **help** to create a 'master race' by teaching Nazi ideas about race.
It was a **way** of spreading propaganda and ideas.

86 Nazi youth groups

Similarities:
Taught **Nazi** racial ideas
Focus **on** health and sport
Taught **about** greatness of Germany
Taught **about** Hitler
Lots of **outdoor** activities.
Differences:
Boys **taught** military skills
Girls **taught** how to look after the home
Girls **taught** about looking after children
Boys' **groups** later used for recruiting for the military
Boys' **groups** did a lot to support the war effort.

87 Economic changes

Ways include:
Jobs **were** created through public works.
Increased trade and production, and so increased jobs.
Rearmament increased jobs.
More people recruited to the army.
Jews **and** women who'd been dismissed from their jobs weren't counted.
Opponents were in concentration camps, so weren't counted.
National Labour Service was compulsory and took people out of the figures.

88 German people's lives

Reasons that support the statement:
Some Germans benefitted as employment did rise.
Wages rose.
Some working conditions did improve.
Strength through Joy provided leisure activities.
Farmers benefitted as food prices rose.
Big business benefitted as trades unions were abolished; businesses were supported by rearmament and subsidies.
Reasons that don't support the statement:
Some women resented losing their jobs.
Jewish people found life increasingly difficult as discrimination turned to persecution.
Cost of living increased.
Workers had few rights.
Working hours increased.

89 Ideas and policies on race

The Nazis believed that different races were of different value, and that Aryans were the best or 'master race'. They believed that other races were inferior – especially Slavs, black people and gypsies, and that Jews were the lowest race of all. Not all Aryans were part of the master race, though. The mentally ill, disabled, homosexuals and vagrants were not acceptable either.

90 Treatment of Jews, 1933–39

Examples include:
Violence increased (from limited violence in the 1933 boycott of Jewish shops to the more widespread violence of Kristallnacht in 1938).
Attacks on property (some windows smashed in the 1933 boycott of Jewish shops, then widespread destruction of Jewish property in Kristallnacht).
Loss of livelihood (Jews sacked from more and more types of job – e.g. 1933, government jobs; 1935, army; 1936, vets and teachers; 1938, doctors – who could now only treat other Jews).
Not allowed to run businesses; their businesses were taken over; loss of freedoms (1934, banned from public places; 1935, Nuremburg Laws denied Jews citizenship, so they lost the right to vote).

91 Treatment of Jews, 1939–45

Examples include:
In occupied countries Jews were forced into ghettos in cities where few supplies were allowed in and many starved or died of disease.
More were taken to concentration camps in Germany (e.g. Bergen-Belsen) and elsewhere where conditions were awful and they were made to work very hard.
After Germany invaded Russia, killing squads began to round up Jews in Russian towns.
After 1942, Jews were transported to death camps in Poland (e.g. Treblinka, Auschwitz); most of them were killed in gas chambers in these camps when they arrived.

UNIT 3: SOURCE SKILLS

92 Source skills 1

(a) For inference questions (Q1 on the exam paper): you should give two things you can learn from the source and support each one with reference to the source and an explanation of how it supports the inference.

(b) For analysis questions (Q2 on the exam paper): you should identify the message that the artist or author of the source is trying to get across. You also need to explain and give examples of how they do this, for example through what they have chosen to include and chosen to leave out, their use of language and the details included for written sources or their choice of colour and the way they've positioned objects or people for visual sources.

93 Source skills 2

(a) For cross-referencing questions (Q3 on the exam paper): you need to give examples of ways the sources agree and disagree with each other and then come to a judgement about how far they agree. You need to weigh up the evidence on both sides so you can reach a judgement.

(b) For usefulness or reliability questions (Q4 on the exam paper): you need to look at the content of each of the sources and come to a judgement on how useful this content is for the historian's enquiry. You then need to decide how reliability might affect the value of the content of the sources and then decide which source is more useful.

94 Source skills 3

For the evaluation of a hypothesis question (Q5 on the exam paper): you need to go through the sources carefully and use your own knowledge to plan your answer. Organise your answer to look at those sources that support and those that don't support the hypothesis, using your own knowledge to add details. Finally, you should explain why the evidence is stronger on one side than the other and come to a conclusion. For top marks, you should also consider the reliability of the sources in your answer.

UNIT 3A: SOURCE SKILLS

95 Dealing with pain

The purpose of Source A is to spread the news of a new anaesthetic – chloroform – and persuade doctors to use it. The author tries to do this by writing in a well-known medical journal that other doctors would read. The title of the article sets out his intentions – comparing chloroform favourably with ether, which was already being used in operations. The author uses persuasive language – 'greatly less quantity', 'more rapid and complete', 'strongly declare'.

96 Dealing with infection

Source B shows that:
The floor and shelves are very clean and tidy.
Clean sheets are covering surfaces, stopping germs spreading.
Equipment is covered – indicating that it's been sterilised.
Nurses are wearing very clean gowns.
Nurses are wearing face masks to stop infection passing from them onto wounds.
Nurses are wearing caps to stop infection passing from their hair.
Nurses are wearing rubber gloves, so as not to pass germs from their hands onto instruments or the patient.
There are no spectators or anyone other than medical staff in the room.

97 Dealing with blood loss

Useful because: it's evidence doctors were carrying out blood transfusions at this time; it shows the procedure itself – via arteries using tourniquets etc; shows that another person needed to be present to take the blood from; shows that it was quite a straightforward procedure because there's only one doctor present.
Not useful because: it doesn't give any information on whether the transfusion worked; doesn't show how widespread the practice of transfusions was; doesn't give any information about who the volunteer donating blood is and therefore how people became donors; doesn't give any information on the patient's condition – why she needed a transfusion.

98 Influencing factors

The author of Source D thinks Gillies was a very important surgeon and pioneer of plastic surgery, and this is communicated through the language used both in showing what other surgeons were doing – 'stitched the edges', 'leaving men's faces to become twisted and horribly disfigured' – and in the suggestion that Gillies' methods were better: 'pioneered new treatments', 'reconstruct', 'cannot be underestimated'.

UNIT 3B: SOURCE SKILLS

99 The General Strike

Origin of Source A: Written by J. Wilkes in 1984.
Nature of Source A: social and economic history book. Suggests that it's unlikely the author was involved in the events, and historians usually try to give a balanced view. However, the title of the book does suggest that it focuses on the workers, rather than the government. The account itself shows that there were mixed opinions within the TUC. However, we don't know who J. Wilkes is or what his political views are, so we can't be completely sure of its reliability.

100 The miners' strike

The large number of police shown indicates that lots of police were used to patrol the picket line, which in turn suggest that lots of miners were on strike and picketing. It looks as though a physical struggle is taking place between pickets and police, indicating violence. The caption says a man was killed, indicating that the violence was quite bad. The number of people and the suggested violence show that passions were high on both sides; the caption says that the man killed was not from Nottinghamshire, indicating that he was a 'flying picket'.

101 Suffragettes

The purpose of the poster in Source C is to win support for the Suffragettes by showing that women were being force fed in prison and how awful force-feeding was.
The ways the artist gets the message across are:
Prisoner looks in pain and is struggling – the chair is being lifted off the floor.
There are a large number of people holding her down.
It shows the way that force feeding was done – tube through the nose and liquid food being poured down.
The impression given by the prison wardens – looking scary, hard and unsympathetic.
The writing on the poster emphasising that the Suffragettes saw themselves as 'political' prisoners, which meant they should not be treated cruelly.
It shows the strength of the woman and how much she believes in the cause because she's willing to go through this horrible treatment.

102 Poll tax protests

Ways in which Source D would be useful for a historian: it describes a range of methods of protests used; it indicates that non-payment was the most successful method; it suggests numbers of people involved.
Ways in which Source D wouldn't be useful: description of the methods is only brief – would need more information, for example, where protest marches took place, who organised them, where they were held, etc. Focuses on methods used in Scotland – would need other evidence for England and Wales.

Published by Pearson Education Limited, Edinburgh Gate, Harlow, Essex, CM20 2JE.

www.pearsonschoolsandfecolleges.co.uk

Copies of official specifications for all Edexcel qualifications may be found on the Edexcel website: www.edexcel.com

Text © Pearson Education Limited 2013
Edited by Wearset Ltd, Boldon, Tyne and Wear
Typeset by Tech-Set Ltd, Gateshead
Original illustrations © Pearson Education Limited 2013
Illustrated by KJA Artists
Cover illustration by Miriam Sturdee

The rights of Kirsty Taylor to be identified as author of this work have been asserted by her in accordance with the Copyright, Designs and Patents Act 1988.

First published 2013

16 15 14 13
10 9 8 7 6 5 4 3 2 1

British Library Cataloguing in Publication Data
A catalogue record for this book is available from the British Library

ISBN 978 1 446 90514 2

Printed in Slovakia by Neografia

Acknowledgements
The publisher would like to thank the following for their kind permission to reproduce their photographs:

(Key: b-bottom; c-centre; l-left; r-right; t-top)

akg-images Ltd: 41; **Alamy Images:** Classic Image 4l, GL Archive 76cl, INTERFOTO 82, Mary Evans Picture Library 7t, 83r, 89, North Wind Picture Archives 45, 48, 49, 53, 58, 61, The Art Gallery Collection 2, The Print Collector 27; **Bridgeman Art Library Ltd:** 28b, English Heritage Photo Library 37, Look and Learn 28t, Peter Newark American Pictures 47, Universal History Archive / UIG 90, 95b; **Canterbury Archaeological Trust Ltd:** 14; **Fotolia.com:** JulietPhotography 16; **Getty Images:** Photodisc 34, Popperfoto 22, Science and Society Picture Library 96t, The Bridgeman Art Library / John Gast 51, Universal Images Group 95c; **Great Ormond Street Hospital:** 8t, 8b; **Mary Evans Picture Library:** 50, 101, Epic / Tallandier 91, Everett Collection 54, Imagno 72, 76cr, INTERFOTO / Sammlung Rauch 25, Metropolitan Police Authority 29, Sueddeutsche Zeitung Photo 76b, 80; **PhotoDisc:** 64; **Photoshot Holdings Limited:** 78, UPPA / Dylan Martinez 32; **Randall Bytwerk:** 84; **www.reportdigital.co.uk:** John Sturrock 100; **Science Photo Library Ltd:** 7b, National Library of Medicine 21, Photo Researchers 20, St. Bartholomew's Hospital 96; **Shutterstock.com:** mishabender 1, 15t, 15b; **SuperStock:** Science and Society 97; **TopFoto:** Fotomas 26, HIP 43, Roger-Viollet 74, The Granger Collection 55; **Ullstein Bild:** AKG / Witterstein 83l; **Wellcome Library, London:** 4r

All other images © Pearson Education Limited

We are grateful to the following for permission to reproduce copyright material:
Newsquest Media Group Limited for an extract from 'Hospital reveals faces of battle' by Linda Piper in *News Shopper*, 23 November 2007 www.newsshopper.co.uk. Reproduced with permission; and Cambridge University Press for an extract from *United Kingdom: A Social and Economic History of Modern Britain* by John Wilkes, 1984. Reproduced by permission.

Every effort has been made to contact copyright holders of material reproduced in this book. Any omissions will be rectified in subsequent printings if notice is given to the publishers.

In the writing of this book, no Edexcel examiners authored sections relevant to examination papers for which they have responsibility.